You Can Look but
DON'T TOUCH

A Real-Life Game Changer for Single Women!

KEEBE SMITH

ARCHWAY
PUBLISHING

Archway Publishing books may be ordered through booksellers or by contacting:

Archway Publishing
1663 Liberty Drive
Bloomington, IN 47403
www.archwaypublishing.com
1 (888) 242-5904

Because of the dynamic nature of the Internet, any web addresses or
links contained in this book may have changed since publication and
may no longer be valid. The views expressed in this work are solely those
of the author and do not necessarily reflect the views of the publisher,
and the publisher hereby disclaims any responsibility for them.

Any people depicted in stock imagery provided by Thinkstock are models,
and such images are being used for illustrative purposes only.
Certain stock imagery © Thinkstock.

ISBN: 978-1-4808-2071-5 (sc)
ISBN: 978-1-4808-2072-2 (e)

Library of Congress Control Number: 2015948845

Print information available on the last page.

Archway Publishing rev. date: 10/8/2015

CONTENTS

ROMANS 12:1 (NKJV)

I BESEECH YOU THEREFORE, brethren, by the mercies of God, that you present your bodies a living sacrifice, holy, acceptable to God, which is your reasonable service.

DEDICATION

This book is dedicated to the following:

Drs. Mike and Dee Dee Freeman, for covering me, teaching me the Word of God and setting an example for me that is unparalleled to that of others. You have, without question, modeled "what faith and a man can do!"

Pastor Dewayne Freeman, for dissecting the Word of God in a simplistic manner, yet with great revelation. You and the Word of God are a lethal combination!

Dad, "The Coolest Man in the Land." Thank you for teaching me the value of moderation and preparation. You taught me that acquiring a blessing is only one dimension-maintenance is equally important. Forever your "Shorty."

Mommy, for being a living example of the Word in action. Words are limited when it comes to describing who you are to me. Thank you for trusting God through it all, setting an example of godliness as a woman, mother and wife and for being my "Best Friend Forever!"

Conrad "Connie," for showing me a godly example of a dad, man and husband. You raised the bar. Thank you for making me "Connie's Baby."

Chayah, for being everything I could have dreamed of in a daughter.

Navi, for being "mommy's baby boy" and whose very life has strengthened my faith in God.

Monkeydo, for being my real life superhero! Your love alone has set a lifelong impression that cannot be forgotten.

Quan, for being my most faithful and only member and for blessing me with one more great cousin.

Aunt Buddy, for being my biggest cheerleader.

Poopie, for capturing every moment and memory that connects us as family. You are so special to me!

Bukhari, for the relationship that we have as cousins. We smile on purpose!

Libby for being the best big cousin ever and for giving me the best godbaby ever!

Enje, for hanging in there with me from the pit to the promise! We surpassed "ride or die."

Terri White, for loving me the way you do. You invested in my spiritual life like I was your own and I am forever grateful for that.

Kym Harden, if found in the dictionary it would be defined as "soldier, warrior and gangsta in Christ." Thank you for staying on the front line for me.

Cookie, for modeling holy living before me while you were a single woman. You have been an amazing big sister and woman of God.

Ma Nina and Uncle Rick, for always reminding me of who I am in Christ and for your many prayers.

Ma Olga, for being the most supportive, "milk and cookies," mother I could ever have.

Alek and Thanh, for being the absolute best big brother and sister that God could ever bless me with.

Ms. Jones, for being so instrumental during my journey. Thank you

My girlfriends (Taci, Monica, Beulah, Jennifer, Matielyn and Latricia,), for embracing me as God's daughter and accepting me as your friend. I love y'all chicks.

Marginette Alison, for allowing God to use you during a major transformation in my life. I know you love me!

Lisa, for never ceasing to believe that I was going to fulfill the call of God on my life. My little sister for life!

To ALL my young people, for reminding me that you need to see an example of something different and I am that difference!

FOREWORD

As I LOOK AT my mother, I see change, growth and the uncommon. She has transformed her mindset and lifestyle for the better. God has given my mom revelation on how to live holy as a single woman and find herself in Him. She has been a great role model and my mindset has shifted from what seems like the impossible to what now seems possible to me. "You Can Look but Don't Touch" isn't just some catchy slogan; it is a renewed mindset for women. Ladies, I am not saying this because I think it might work. I am watching it work in my mom's life every day!

CHAYAH NORRIS, DAUGHTER, 15 YRS. OLD

PREFACE

FOLLOWING YEARS OF HURT, pain, confusion and chaos, I allowed God to show me how He has called me to live as a single woman. After experiencing freedom and peace in this journey, I was clear that my responsibility was to empower, encourage and educate other women with the very same revelation given to me.

CHAPTER 1

Welcome to My World

••

I come to you with full transparency concerning my journey and my God given revelation. This is done with one purpose in mind: that women will embrace the peace, promises, protection and preparation that is available to us with living free! I am a believer in Jesus Christ and I will include Biblical references that God used to teach me during my awesome experience with Him. However, I must repeat the words of my Assistant Pastor Dewayne Freeman, "Don't merely believe what I say but search the Word of God for yourself!"

To get a real sense of my background, I am going to share some of my history. I am a single parent with two wonderful teenagers that I love so much. I am saved, educated and an ordained minister of the Gospel of Jesus Christ. By profession, I serve in the field of education. While all that sounds good; here is the real deal. I am a single woman currently living in my freedom but I was a CERTIFIED MESS in my past.

I grew up in a two parent household for the first five years of my life. Five was a very critical age in my life because it was at that time my parents separated and I became the victim of sexual abuse. The abuse lasted for the next three years and those two events shaped me more than others or even I realized. After my parents separated, I had a very strained relationship with my father and at the same time my body was being violated constantly by a family member. I never shared with anyone concerning the abuse so I was left to deal with its effects on my own. You can guess how effective I was with dealing with the matter, considering my very young age. Well, let's move forward to my teenage years. I was officially being raised in a single parent home, however afforded many opportunities and experiences nonetheless. I attended private schools, participated in extracurricular activities and was active in my church. My mother worked very hard at trying to keep me from experiencing the effects of being raised in a single parent home but it didn't work in its entirety. I was taught to be well behaved, articulate and poised. I learned very early the value of public presentation. I was skilled at smiling, sitting up straight, crossing my legs at the ankle and greeting with a soft and pleasant tone. The downfall was, my public presentation was not an accurate representation of my private struggle. I was hurting, scared, confused, pissed off, insecure and yet, I held those feelings in with a smile.

Those experiences created dysfunctional survival techniques. I was determined to avoid hurt, rejection, abandonment and disappointment at all cost. Even if it meant, I hurt you before you hurt me! Those feelings did not discriminate. I didn't trust females any more than I did males. I didn't know who to trust and because of that, I placed everyone in the same category. They all appeared to be candidates for the same type of abuse, disappointment and rejection I had experienced. I lived a very guarded life. I learned quickly that if I smiled and laughed, people rarely realized that I wasn't talking or letting them into my world. I created a very strict checklist for lowering my walls. It became very important for me to be emotionally and physically safe. I was also convinced that I was the only one willing to provide that. Well, I entered into my young adult years and by then I was a "doozy" to say the least. My mother had remarried by then and I was blessed with a great dad. However, the damage in my life was already done and I was in need of a lot of repair. I didn't know why I handled people or life the way I did; I just knew I had a real unique way of thinking and behaving.

Well as time passed, I had graduated to being that "chick!" I was "two dollar" cute with a dimple and a big smile. Let's remember a two dollar bill is a rare find! I was well liked by many, but especially men. I was that woman that men wanted to take home to "Mama." Little did they know, they should have been running when they saw me coming. I was literally on the prowl. I was extremely social, yet reserved and determined to be that player chick! My motivation wasn't that I just desired playing games, but it was fueled from a need to fill a void. Stick with me and I will explain. I grew up with an uncle that I absolutely adored and admired. He was everything to me in the body of a man. One of the many things that I admired was his hypnotizing effect on women. Growing up, I watched how he was able to use his words, body language and charming personality to get them to do and say just what he wanted. That amazed me and at the age of 14, I silently decided that I wanted that skill. I started to study him. When I was around him, which was always, it was no longer just about us spending time together but I was on an assignment to learn. See, I figured out early on that if I could manipulate a person's way of thinking, I could control what happened to me, or so I thought. How wrong! See, I was still operating in the "head space" of that broken little girl who was sexually abused, scared, confused, hurting and simply wanted to be loved and protected. However, I needed a strategy to make it happen. Well, after years of studying my uncle I was ready to go to work! So, when I tell you I was that chick, it's not an understatement. I was running game from every angle. I was clear about one thing: men recognized a woman's game but very few men recognized a man's game being played by a woman! I used the very same techniques men used because I was trained by a man. Once I learned that, it was on! Now, for clarity and correlating purposes, I want you to understand what I was after. I was never after money, that wasn't my need. As stated previously, my family took very good care of me so I never needed or wanted a man for money. I wanted their minds and hearts and that's what I worked for. I wanted the very things I missed out on as a child. It was my intent to have multiple men consumed with me. Having just one man was too "chancy," so I aimed for multiple.

My background is in psychology, education and counseling. Therefore, I was knowledgeable concerning the power of the mind. So, while other women were attempting to get the hearts of men, I was working to capture their minds. I knew that if I got their minds, everything else would work to my advantage. I would officially be in control of what happens in the relationship. That's how the mind works. Come on women, think about the many times we have no longer been feeling a man emotionally but continued to do or be there for him. That was a result of our minds, not our hearts. I wanted the same thing. I wasn't looking to hurt anyone. I was looking to guarantee the love, protection and stability that I had rarely experienced from men coming up. Since that was my agenda, my social life reflected just that. I was like a dealer attempting to create addicts. Oddly enough, sex was not my hook. I understood early that men could get sex anywhere. I also felt I wasn't a true player chick if I used sex as my hook because the average woman could do that. I created this idea in my head that if you can create an "addict" without sex then you're really a bad chick. This is not to say that we didn't eventually have sex but it wasn't my "go to." Mentally twisted, I know! No, I took a different approach. I studied them to identify what they lacked, wanted or even needed. I then worked to provide just that. I catered, encouraged, complimented, supported –attempted to provide exactly what they needed. I was good to them, but for all the wrong reasons. I wanted to provide an experience for them that was so addictive that they worked to provide what I was in need of. Once they were hooked, I felt a sense of security and I would begin that same process with the next person. This cycle did overlap and "yes," I was using that strategy on multiple men at the same time. I was feeding on the attention and preoccupation they demonstrated towards me after being hooked. I desperately wanted the assurance that I was wanted, cared for, protected and loved. I was determined to get what I missed coming up. Now you may be saying, "what about your uncle?" Yes, he was everything and some more but he was not my dad. Nothing can replace what a dad's love and involvement can provide.

Now, let's back up a tad bit. I accepted Jesus as my Lord and Savior at 14 years old. I was consistently in church on Sunday and Bible study with my mother. Don't judge me. I know you're thinking, "I can't tell!" Remember, salvation traded my old spirit for a new one, but it did not change my mind. We are responsible for renewing our minds and as you can tell, mine was not renewed at that time.

As previously shared, growing up I was exposed to the Word of God. Therefore, I knew that my lifestyle was not God's best for me. The manipulation, the games, the multiple dudes and that craving for love, attention and stability in the wrong places was out of control. It was never enough. Guys would tell me that I was worse than a dude and yet some were mesmerized by the skill. It wasn't long after college that I really decided to work on my relationship with God. I knew that there was a God-given purpose for my life and it wasn't to run game on men, although I was demonstrating mastery in that area. During that time, I met a young man at a church revival service, although I was at the service with the man I was currently dating. I secretly received his phone number, without either man knowing, and left the church service. As you can tell, I had a long way to go and grow. That spirit was still fighting to stay alive. I told y'all we are responsible for renewing our minds. God will not do that for you! I eventually married the young man that I secretly met. He was a man of God, ordained minister and was very sincere in his interest concerning me. Well, I married at the tender age of 22, had my daughter at 24 and my son at 25. I was already pregnant with my son at my six weeks checkup. *Go figure!*....That marriage was a huge mistake, but I was blessed with two kids. As the ole folks say, "I wasn't bit mo ready for marriage." I was spiritually and naturally too immature for a covenant of that magnitude but I didn't realize it at the time. That is not to say that all 22 year olds aren't prepared for marriage, but I wasn't. There was still so much work and transformation needed within me and marriage did not mix well with that baggage. I was really trying to pull it together spiritually and I had some good runs but the consistency was a struggle. Hebrews 13:7 talks about how there should be a consistency that runs through us all. After a period of becoming more serious about the things of God, I was ordained as a minister at 27 years old. God revealed to me at the age of 20 that there was a call on my life. As a result, I was not shocked about the ordination just concerned because I knew that even with my growth I still had a lot of residue from childhood and adult life that had to be addressed. I started periodically teaching and preaching the gospel when opportunities arose, but life still wasn't quite right for me. Not too long after this, that spirit that I was entertaining prior to marriage rose up during my marriage and infidelity was one of my unfortunate contributions. There was so much confusion and chaos in my life that it was utterly ridiculous. I even continued in the relationship with the man from the affair. Efforts were made to weather the storm, but in my heart, I really didn't want to. We separated after five years of marriage and then eventually divorced.

Unfortunately, I misled the man I was having the affair with as well. He was led to believe that after the divorce we would proceed as a couple and live happily ever after. So he patiently waited! I was legally divorced and officially on the scene again. Oh No!

I was in my early thirties, divorced, still "two dollar" cute with a dimple and "doing me!" I had a house, two luxury cars, degrees, a decent paying job, traveling and living like pure Hell! What an oxymoron. That is truly what life was like for me. See, despite the hellish lifestyle I was living, I had enough Word in me and enough of a relationship with God to know that my living was out of order. I was dating who I wanted, when I wanted, how many I wanted and do know these were not Bible Study dates. I was officially back in that same place, entertaining that same spirit. I just didn't know that I was attempting to fill a void. I just thought that I was a bad chick and knew how to handle men better than others. I was living the formula that the world teaches women. You know, "Do You," "Turn Up" but they fail to tell you what happens after. There are consequences that hunt you down after you indulge in that tantalizing lifestyle of hidden chaos. In between those episodes of "straight pimpin," I attempted to have some exclusive relationships. How simple was that? I was merely attracting the same caliber of foolishness that was residing in me. Nevertheless, you can already predict how those relationships started and ended. It was the typical heartache, heartbreak, drama-filled endings that would have met the criteria for any here and now reality show. The craziest part of it was that the men brought the drama. I am by nature a very reserved, laid back, drama-free type woman. I don't like hollering, fussing, cussing and the like. So, they were the culprits acting ridiculous. However, we must remember that I was attracting men with their own set of issues on top of what I brought to the relationship. Terrible Combination!

During this time, my spirit and flesh were truly in a battle. I was still struggling with my social life while also knowing that God had called me to live according to His Word. I was never confused about the standard I was supposed to be living by. The disconnect occurred because a portion of me still wanted to entertain that lifestyle and I was also spiritually knowledgeable but weak because my lifestyle catered to my flesh, not my spirit. I was in a jam or at least I thought I was. However, God being awesome has always used Holy

Spirit to convict, correct and guide me. When I identified that I was going to entertain that lifestyle again, I went to my Pastor at the time and requested to be sat down as a minister. I was crystal clear that I was not living holy and under no circumstance was I going to preach something that I was not living! I hope you are really seeing this picture and how chaotic it was.

Well, let's travel to my mid-thirties. A chick was TIRED! I was tired of crying, the drama and being hurt in those unhealthy relationships. I was also tired of dealing with "nutball" dudes (my definition: that space saver man that does not compliment you in any capacity but does what is needed to fill the temporary space/void in your life). I was tired of playing pimp chick when in my heart I knew I wanted a healthy relationship. I was tired of lying at the altar every Sunday morning begging God to make it all stop. *Disclaimer: God will NOT make stuff stop, but He has empowered us to make stuff start and stop!* I was tired of feeling like God was disappointed in me because I knew better. Tired of feeling like God was simply tolerating me, which was farthest from the truth, but I didn't know that at the time. Sin will cloud your perception of God. I was tired y'all. Tired of trying to live holy but falling in that same sin all over again! That life was wearing me out.

Now, don't get it twisted, on the outside I looked the part. You know, that look the world gives you credit for. It's the look that causes those without discernment to think that you "got it made." I mastered that look. Hair done, nails and toes manicured, designer bags, high heels and ready to step out for the day. Chick was straight faking it! Why, you ask? I was internally miserable. I was spending most nights crying over something a dude did or because of my disappointment in myself concerning my relationship with God. I knew with everything in me that I deserved to live a better life. I was completely convinced that God had more for me and that I wasn't created to live according to the common standards set by this world for women.

I can vividly remember, I was in my house one night and it was about 11 p.m. The man I was in a relationship with had just left and I went back to my bedroom (yes, because that's where we had just departed from). I said to God, "I'm done living like this, I will be abstinent until marriage." Now, be clear, the man and I didn't have any argument or issue prior, but when he walked out that door my spirit said, "It is over," and I embraced that statement with a "yes." Now for people who know me, they know that I am a selective communicator. I am verbal when I want to be! So, the next morning I called the man and casually said, "I'm not having sex anymore." He panicked. He began to ask why, what was going on? Hilarious! Dude, I didn't say your oxygen supply was going to be cut, I said "no more sex." Well, I understood that it felt the same to him. He attempted to be patient with the change but I knew that the relationship would eventually fade out and I was internally grateful. I was also clear that he was going to start getting it from somewhere else. This is not to say that men will not honor that standard but I knew he wasn't the dude that would. After that conversation, I called a girlfriend who is an awesome woman of God, married and also walked the journey I was about to embark. I shared with her what I had done and asked would she be my accountability partner. Of course, she agreed. I knew that accountability would be crucial to maintaining sexual purity and integrity.

Well, I'm in this new place in life and trying to figure out "now what?" This place was not without error because I did fall once more but after that, I not only determined to remain abstinent but to embark on a journey of getting to know myself. I was clear that I had to learn more about myself and the only way to do so was to learn more about God. If I didn't, I would continue to end up in the scenarios that led to that lifestyle. I needed to know what made me tick, why I was attracted to certain types of men, why I required the things I did from men and what things were assisting me in getting into those compromising situations. These are some of the questions that I needed answers to and ASAP. Jeremiah 1:5 (NKJV) says, "Before I formed you in the womb I knew you." So who better to ask than God? More was needed than just a commitment to abstinence. I needed understanding as to who I really was. I also needed a blueprint for living holy as a single woman and I was convinced that God had all the information. Now, just like many others, I was raised in church and grew up hearing "No sex until marriage," but I was in great need of more than that statement. Not only was that a rarity, but I knew very few around me who were living that life or did prior to marriage. I needed someone that could walk with me during this time other than my one married girlfriend. Don't fret, God wasn't busy and still isn't!

Ladies, as much as I am constantly grateful for the love of God demonstrated in my life, I too want you to experience His love at another level. We all have our stories. Your story may not include strained relationships, rejection, abandonment or sexual abuse. Your story may include alcoholism, drug abuse, sickness, violence, the fear of failure, never feeling good enough, qualified, etc. Regardless of the area, we all have our stuff. Psalm 51:5 (NKJV) says, "Behold, I was brought forth in iniquity, and in sin my mother conceived me." We entered in this world in a position of needing the Almighty God. So often we put those things behind us and just do life as is. We go through our daily routine of work, church, raising kids, sharing hobbies, but as much as we have placed the less pleasant things behind us, it doesn't mean they aren't affecting us. The world's concept of success can be so deceiving. It can lead people to believe that they are doing well because they are acquiring and maintaining "stuff." That theory is so far from the truth. For so many years, I had not a clue that the experiences from my childhood had a major impact on how I viewed life and myself in general. Those things had laid a foundation for how I spoke, thought, behaved, what concerned me and those things I thought I needed. However, because I learned to manage my daily routine in a responsible manner it gave the perception that I was doing well. I wasn't. Managing a daily routine is important; demonstrating responsibility is important, but being "whole" surpasses both. I was pursuing a career, got married, had children and yet there was still an empty place in my life. That is not how God has called us to live. He has so much more for us than that. John 10:10b (NKJV) says, "I have come that they may have life, and that they may have it more abundantly." I was fine according to the world's standards, but I was living beneath my privilege according to the kingdom of God! How many of you are living beneath the Word of God? Yes, you are paying bills, climbing the corporate ladder, taking the kids to practice, serving at church on Sunday, helping your family, traveling and always on the go. Your life is busy, busy, busy. My pastor has taught us not to mistake movement with progress. Just because you're moving doesn't mean you're making progress. He used the illustration of a merry go round. It is indeed moving but it isn't going anywhere. Well, I don't know where you are today, but that's what my life was like for a very long time – I was moving constantly but going nowhere. This is your moment. You have the power to determine what you will create in this moment. This can be just another book reading that stirs you up for a few days or even a week, only to return to life as usual. Or, you can read this book with the intent that God is going to transform your life and this is but one resource that He will use in the process. I say this because I was the "queen" of reading a great book, watching a movie, DVD or attending a powerful service that had me excited about changing the quality of my life; yet not long after, I would return to my previous way of doing or thinking. My pastor constantly teaches us that "We live and die by the choices we make." You can decide today that this will not just be another good read. You can decide at this very moment in time that you need God and in a way that you have not yet experienced. He knows exactly where you have been, what you have experienced, where you are right now and where you are destined to go. So who better to include in this experience? We often turn to family, friends or outside vices to help us through this thing called life. Some work, some eat, some drink, have sex, party, some worry and the like, but God wants us to rely on Him and Him alone. He desires to be our life source; not our education, looks, skillset, money, friends or family. There is a story in the Bible where Jesus was speaking to the multitudes and yet He went straight gangsta at one point after being told that His mother and brothers were waiting to speak to Him. His response was, "But He answered and said to the one who told Him, "Who is My mother and who are My brothers?" And He stretched out His hand toward His disciples and said, "Here are My mother and My brothers! For whoever does the will of My Father in heaven is My brother and sister and mother." (Matthew 12:48-50 NKJV) Jesus wasn't being disrespectful concerning his mama, so all you mamas' calm down. However, Jesus was making the distinction that it wasn't about His natural bloodline. It was about the relationship with God and how all those focused on the same are His family. We have to be connected to likeminded people. This walk requires changing your focus, possibly changing your people and how you manage your time. What do I mean? In order to walk with Jesus and allow Him to change your life, it requires time with Him. It requires consulting Him, including Him, eliminating the mentality of "just doing" stuff. Is "just doing" working for you? If not, stop and start following. Begin following His lead and watch where you end up. It will be the best change you could ever make! Trust me on this one. Jesus is waiting for you to invite Him into this place of your life. You may have accepted Him as Lord and Savior of your life but we also have the ability to only allow Him to be Lord in certain domains. Crazy right? Here is a personal example: I have been tithing since I was a teenager. I was taught the principle, received revelation and began implementing the practice and never stopped. I decided to trust God with my money and as an adult it didn't matter what was due or if I had a major need. It was not going to hinder me from paying my tithe and giving an offering. Well, it is an understatement to say that I am so grateful that I have obeyed this principle because as His Word says, "And I will rebuke the devourer for your sake" (Malachi 3:10 NKJV) and this is not limited to the financial arena. However, for many years of my life I did not invite God in nor trust Him with my social life. I would try in my own strength to do it God's way but I struggled for years with completely turning my hand over to God. What's the difference? I knew how I was supposed to live, I understood the principles, but obeyed in one area and disobeyed in another. Why? I didn't really trust that He would take care of me in that area. Notice I said "would" not "could." I knew that He could but I used to struggle with whether God would do certain things for me. Trust is the main factor. You know the areas that you rely on God and the ones you have been taking care of on your own. A good way to determine those areas is by looking at the outcomes. Look at your level of peace when they don't seem to go the way you are expecting. Anything God calls for, He provides for and there is peace in that. Examine how much is required of you to make it happen. Examine how much faith is required to see it manifest. If it is something you can do, then it probably is YOU. When God is involved, there is a peace that surpasses all understanding. There is also a true demonstration of His existence in the very matter that cannot be confused. I heard a minister say recently that you cannot tell him what God said if you don't know His Word. Wow...I love that. He said, "You cannot distinguish between the language and voice of God if you do not already have a relationship with His voice, which is crystal clear through His Word. How do we know if something is from God if we are not meditating on His Word? This is so true. I can remember a time when I was doing youth ministry and my young people had a birthday party for me. All who know me know that I love a birthday. During the party they passed out a worksheet that had maybe six or seven of my most quoted sayings. Each saying had a word or two missing. The goal of the assignment was to see who knew me best. The majority of my young people answered correctly. They knew how I spoke because they spent time with me and listened to what I had to say, likewise with Jesus. This journey will require that we learn how He speaks, what He has done and who He is. This is the road map to us living the abundant life here on earth. If we are not hearing His voice for direction or following His example for navigating through life, then who are we listening too? And why? We do have another option. Make a decision right now to completely surrender to God and to allow Jesus to truly be Lord over your life.

ASSIGNMENT:

SPEND SOME UNINTERRUPTED QUIET time just thinking about the quality of your life. If you have not accepted Jesus as your Lord and Savior then do that now. *(Turn to the appendix for the Prayer of Salvation).* If you are saved but know that you are not living the life that God has called you to live, then take this moment to tell Him just that. Ask God to show you how to change your life so that it lines up with the plan He has for you.

DISCLAIMER:

CHANGE CAN BE UNCOMFORTABLE at times and can create all types of feelings, but whatever you do, don't flee from this moment. The outcome that lies behind the discomfort is far greater than the temporary feelings you may encounter. Don't jump ship because the boat begins to rock, you're headed to a place of paradise here on earth! Call me when you get here. Love you ladies!

CHAPTER 2

Locate Yourself

..

WHO ARE YOU? WHAT'S important to you? Who or what is the determining factor behind the choices you make? Where have you obtained the standards or principles that you live by? What do you like, want or need? Are you getting what you deserve and want out of friendships and relationships with the opposite sex? Are you experiencing true success as a single? Is this really how or who you are? Or is this what life, previous or current situations shaped you into? Or are you like I was? Living in a vicious cycle of poor choices and destructive outcomes? I was torn between temporary satisfaction, wishful thinking and a quest for when and how that lifestyle would really come to an end.

If you are anything like I was, then it's time to locate yourself. Oh, and get ready because you are going to have a mind-blowing experience with God that will change your life forever. You will never be the same after this!

KeeBe, what does locating myself look like? Glad you asked. Well, go somewhere with me real quick because I need you to clearly understand why Jesus is needed for this journey. By definition, a GPS is a Global Positioning System used to determine the precise location of a vehicle, person or other asset to which it is attached and it records the position of the asset at regular intervals. Follow me because I'm going somewhere. Your family or loved ones may know some stuff about you; your friends can possibly do a decent job of describing you; however, nobody but

the Almighty God knows exactly where you are in your existence
and I don't limit this to physical existence. He knows what's on
your mind, what concerns you, what makes you doubt, insecure
or even fearful. He is well aware of what you like, need and where
those desires were birthed. He knows the areas that can stay and
the ones that must be abandoned; nobody can locate you at all
times like God! He knows the "Real You" – not the one that life has
shaped. I like this part as well, the reason the GPS device works
is because it is "attached." I could shout right here! The definition
specifies that it is able to detect the location of the vehicle, person
or asset through which it is "attached." Your creator God is auto-
matically attached to you, but the caveat is this: He is a gentleman
and will not force Himself on you. You must invite Him in and
request of Him that He take you on a journey toward locating
yourself and do know that He never says, "No." However, like our
cell phones, we must select the option that says "enable GPS" in
order for our phones to utilize the system. Likewise with God,
enable God to take you on this awesome journey. So for the sake of
this book, GPS will stand for "God's Positioning System" and trust
and believe you will end up on the right path. During this period,
God will begin to reveal things to you that you never thought
about and show you things your finite mind would never consider.
He is just awesome like that. He will connect the dots from your
upbringing and adult life while showing you how to access your
freedom from things that were designed to destroy you. What I
know about myself today is assisting with propelling me into my
tomorrow. You must know the heart of God to truly understand
the necessity of identifying where you have come from, who you
are and where you are going. The plan that God has for your life is
individualized and uniquely designed just for you. As a result, you
cannot mirror the life of anybody else. You can receive wisdom,
tips and insight from others, but the meat of your journey must
be given by God the Father. The Bible says, "It is written, 'Man

shall not live by bread alone, but by every word that proceeds from the mouth of God.'" (Matthew 4:4 NKJV) We need to hear from God and some may be asking: how do I hear from God? Read His Word! His word is His voice speaking directly to you. Start right there. Meditate on His word and you will begin to understand how He sees you, feels about you, how much He loves you and what He has in store for you. Without this information, you will be left to doing life based on how you were raised, what you see others doing and based on what the world dictates. I have a revelation about who I am like never before. I am clear that I am not what I have been through or the product of what I have done. My past has passed! Therefore, if anyone *is* in Christ, *he is* a new creation; old things have passed away; behold, all things have become new. (II Corinthians 5:17 NKJV). My understanding of what I deserve from life has all changed. I am not that broken little girl who was sexually abused or craving a relationship with a father. I am also blessed to say that God has restored the relationship that I have with my biological father. God has taught me the importance of living in this moment and that includes me forgiving, honoring and loving him and I do. I am God's whole and complete daughter.

Watch this: ladies, when you purchase an appliance, if it fails to operate like it should, you don't return it to the shoe store. You contact the makers of the appliance and you share with them what is going wrong. Well, that makes perfect sense because they created the product so they know how it is supposed to work and what to do to get it back to working condition. Ladies, God is your father, your creator and dad. He is more than willing and able to assist you in producing a woman who is not just in working condition, but prospering condition! The world is okay with just meeting the standard, but our God exceeds the standard. The Bible says, "Now to Him who is able to do exceeding abundantly above all that we ask or think, according to the power that works in us." (Ephesians 3:20 NKJV) Ladies, God desires that you exceed abundance in this life. Allow Him to introduce you to yourself! Prosperity in every area of your life is optional. The deciding factor is YOU. God has not chosen some to prosper and others to just make it. For all the mothers of multiple children, we don't look at our children and say, "I want one to do well but I'm ok with the others just barely making it." Who does that? If, as earthly parents, we want the best for our children, just take a moment to imagine how much more God wants for us. He wants all of His children to prosper in every area of our lives and He left us with every resource needed to do so. The Bible says, "as His divine power has given to us all things that *pertain* to life and godliness, through the knowledge of Him who called us by glory and virtue." (II Peter 1:3 NKJV) So if we are living defeated, mundane, routine, "just making it" lifestyles, then that is not based on God's will. It is a result of what we have decided and accepted for our lives. I don't know about you, but I decided that I am entitled to God's best and I will receive it all the days of my life and in every area! I am God's favorite. Now this is where I need you to jump in and say, "No Ma'am, I am God's favorite." You have to begin to get that in your spirit. We live out that which resides in our minds. My pastor has taught us that we must, "visualize, verbalize, internalize and then it will materialize."

Ladies, you deserve to embark on a journey with God that will set you up for prosperity. Why? Because you are His daughter; His favorite; the apple of His eye; the center of His thoughts.

Now let's shift into the practical steps that lend to this journey. I must be transparent in saying that I wish I could tell you that my first effort was praying more or studying the Word more, but it wasn't. I cut off certain people, deleted names and numbers from my phone and stopped dating men. Y'all, I needed a social detox. It was the children, "Fancy" my Maltese, a few girlfriends and my parents. That was officially my circle. This was my new life. Not long after that, I got in contact with the counselor that I had seen years prior. She is absolutely a gift from God. Here I am, 10 years later looking her up to get an appointment. I am a firm believer in counseling. After my first appointment, I knew that this was a critical piece of the journey. I began seeing her regularly. I started spending time just thinking and asking God questions. I would leave my sessions with brand new revelation and I could tell that God was working in me. I was addressing things from childhood, adult life and the list goes on. I was dealing with those very things that helped to shape who I was and yet I was adopting those things that were going to enable me to be who God called me to be. The Bible says that "iron sharpens iron." Yes, I was talking to God more, praying in the spirit more, studying the Word more and reading books/articles on relevant topics. I began experiencing a peace like never before. I also examined things at another dimension, such as: checking my motives, examining my thoughts and responses to situations, exploring whether I was truly hearing from God or simply signing His name to something I wanted. God being so awesome would reveal as quickly as I would ask. It could be anything from conversations with my parents, Him speaking to my spirit, a show I watched, books I read or a sermon ministered. I started keeping CD's of my pastors' teaching in my ear. God definitely uses my pastors to reveal to me – ALWAYS. I have the absolute best pastors in the entire world! Shout out to Drs. Mike and Dee Dee Freeman and Assistant Pastor Dewayne Freeman from the Spirit of Faith Christian Center. They would be ministering and it would seem as if I was the only one in the meeting. Messages were coming forth that divinely spoke to my current situation. Seeds were being sown and with revelation that I had never heard or experienced. I started the process of collecting and applying what I was learning about God and myself at another level. Key word: APPLYING! I was no longer a mere hearer of the Word, as I used to be, which is why there was no consistent demonstration in my life. My desires even changed. I began monitoring my words because, "Death and life *are* in the power of the tongue," (Proverbs 18:21 NKJV). My faith was being increased and I started dreaming again. I was convinced even more that I was not what I did in my past! I am who God says I am and that settled it for me! The more I dove into this journey, the more life just started feeling good! People would ask me sometimes, "Are you lonely, bored or simply, how do you do it?" This time in my life is the very best time I have ever experienced. So let's recap the steps I took: I made a decision to live holy, searched out an accountability partner, asked God to take me on a journey of locating myself and I stopped contacting people who didn't speak the same language and couldn't support my journey (male and female). Dr. Mike always says, "Get with people that have your answer and not your problem." I deleted names and numbers from my phone, started receiving counseling, spent quiet moments thinking, praying, studying the Word, journaling and I kept my pastors' teachings in my ear. My pastor has shared on multiple occasions that he re-evaluates his social circle every six months to see if any changes need to be made. The phenomenal part about God is that He will indeed reveal and expose those that need to stay and those that need to go. My first lady prays a prayer daily that God will expose, reveal and remove. We, however, must be obedient to what He reveals. Now, this is not to say that you need to follow these steps but I would highly recommend it. I can definitely tell you that they have worked for me in an awesome way. God has truly exceeded my expectation in this journey. I wouldn't change one step! See, it was in this place that God began to connect the dots for me concerning why I handled relationships the way I did. He addressed the sexual abuse, the rejection, abandonment and its effects on me. We also dug into the previously strained relationship with my father and my many attempts to fill a void that only God could fill. God specifically knows about your stuff and has a tailor-made plan just for you. You don't have to live with fear, shame, guilt or defeat.

Now, here is the big one for *ME*, and, like I just said, this does not mean it is for *YOU* but it is what I decided. I made a decision to *NEVER* date again! Yes, you read it: *NEVER* date again. Ok, before you say, "That chick has lost it, how is she going to get a husband?" Let me elaborate before your black lace panties get in a knot. Life started becoming so good to me and the peace that I was experiencing was so indescribable that I was seeing life from a different lens. I was receiving life-changing revelation from God. It changed how I viewed myself, relationships and His expectations for me. So, one day I had a conversation with God where I said, "God, I'm not going to date anymore, the next man I entertain will be my husband and in that relationship we will establish a friendship and then move to courtship for the purpose of marriage. I also added that until that time when He reveals my husband to me, I want Him to just continue working on me as a single woman, mother, minister of the gospel of Jesus and soon to be wife. This chick will not be abstinent forever! I tell my girlfriends all the time, the wedding will be an hour and the reception an hour, so don't be late! A chick will have to handle some things. Can I get an Amen? I understand that we have free will and choice. That is a gift from God, but I wanted God to pick my husband. I knew I couldn't go wrong that way. Therefore, I decided to take my hands off of it and shared with God that my husband would be His pick and He would cause him to find me. After he finds me, it is then my responsibility to make a choice to accept him or reject him. I didn't see my request defying any Biblical principles, so it was an established plan between God and myself. Now I understand that people choose their spouses, so don't get technical on me. God gives us that option. I just personally requested that God choose mine. This is NOT to say that you have to do it this way, I am simply sharing the arrangement that I have with God. God is faithful and so I believe that He will honor my prayer! Ladies, we must go to God boldly and make our request known unto him. We are His daughters and it's time we start acting like it. To this day, if there is something I want to do or want from my parents, my mother will immediately say, "girl, you better go ask your father (Conrad) because I am not thinking about you." She's a trip like that, but WOW do I love her! After that is said, I am completely confident that whatever my request is, it is so done! His response is always, "Sure Baby." Don't judge me, I'm still an only child and loving it. Your heavenly father is excited about giving your heart's desires to you, but you must delight in Him, learn who you are according to His Word and discover what's in you. This is how you really identify what you want, need and desire.

Now, the steps I listed may not be for you or they may be. I personally don't want anymore pointless dinners, movies or casual visits. My life has purpose and I only want to entertain the man of God that belongs to me. I don't want a slew of male friends! The next male friend I have will be my husband and I am so okay with that. I am also willing to wait, because my husband is worth that. He is worth me not entertaining men while waiting for his arrival. He is worth me experiencing this awesome journey with God. I am also enjoying this quality time with God during my single years. So no, I have not been out with a man on a date in years. It feels so good to say that, especially based on where I came from. I get to spend my time as a single woman further cultivating my relationship with God, my children, friends and my parents. I do plenty of traveling with my girlfriends and I get to do exciting things like write books and develop programs that will build, encourage and serve people. This is the life I have waited for and it is only getting better.

I have been given the opportunity to work on myself and as a single person, free from the distraction of a relationship. It's just Jesus and me and I love it. I am a firm believer that every single woman needs "alone time." This is not a day, a weekend or some week long retreat in the mountains. I now understand how beneficial it is to separate yourself as much as possible and commune with God for a season. Now, this does not mean that communing with God continuously is not needed, because it is, but this specific type of journey is something different that every single woman should experience. I have also surrounded myself only with girlfriends that speak the same language and support me in my journey. The company we keep is critical both male and female. I don't spend time with these girlfriends often, however, we do communicate for the purpose of fellowship and building each other up. Praise break: I love my life, Thank You Jesus. It is almost impossible to really get in that secret place with God and discover those things as a single woman if you are constantly entertaining a man. Why? Your time is divided, your thoughts are divided, your emotions are divided, but when you remove yourself and it's just you and God, there is a clarity that is experienced in receiving what He reveals like never before. There is a freedom to be vulnerable, the feeling that I have nothing to lose and nowhere to be right now. No afternoon dates, evening check-ins or good night text messages. Now, I am not going to act as if there have not been days where I felt like, "really God? Another weekend with the kids and the dog? 4real God? That feeling doesn't happen often and doesn't last long. It was in some of those moments that I would call my girlfriend and say, "okay, we need to get on a plane; it's vacation time." We would hit an island, swim with some dolphins, watch some shows, laugh, talk and then I was ready to return and resume my normally scheduled programming. Point being, it is beneficial to identify some hobbies, qualified friendships and support systems to have in place for those moments when you feel a little weary in well doing. How about this: It's important to have a LIFE! I'm not talking about working, taking care of home, the kids or helping at church. I'm talking about having a LIFE.

The Bible says, "I have come that they may have life, and that they may have *it* more abundantly. (John 10:10 NKJV). Not, I came that you might just have kids, just have a husband, not just a career, but LIFE! Life is about experiencing abundance in every area. Life includes knowing what you like, enjoying things that interest you, investing in social experiences that allow you to laugh, smile and learn new things. Life is about growing, serving and being a blessing to others. I was faced with the realization a while ago that I knew how to manage my kids, work and church, but outside of that crazy life I had previously lived, I was not experiencing the fullness of life. Ladies, take a class, go to the beach, paint, swim, fly a kite, do something – create a life for yourself! Put the ice cream down, turn the television off and enjoy your life!

If you know that you are in this place of life or one similar, seek God and inquire of Him to see if this type of journey is what you need right now or do what I did and just say, "God, help me to identify who I am in you." See I am clear that Mark 11:24 NKJV tells me, "Therefore I say to you, whatever things you ask when you pray, believe that you receive *them,* and you will have *them..*" So I didn't inquire of Him if it was "the season." I made it the season and with urgency because I needed some immediate changes to manifest in my life. However, you do what you feel is best for you based on God's direction. Although, my suggestion would be, "Honey, boldly go before God and ask Him to escort you through your journey to manifested freedom in Him." We were declared freedom at Calvary and if you have accepted Jesus as your Lord and Savior, you are indeed free. However, being free and experiencing the manifestation of freedom are two different things. It's like being a millionaire but the bank is closed and you can't access any of your money. You are it, but you aren't accessing it! Time out for that in the body of Christ. We will be recipients of the manifestation of the power of God in the earth.

Now, if you decide to continue engaging in relationships with men outside of a courtship then no worries, we will look at how to have healthy friendships in another chapter. They are possible but require some very necessary boundaries and standards. If not, you will be setting yourself up and that chapter of your life is over as of this moment. No more set ups, no more settling; ladies, locate yourselves!

ASSIGNMENT:

TAKE SOME TIME TO think about your life as a single woman. Be honest with yourself and God. He knows regardless. Determine if you're experiencing God's best. If your answer is "No" to either question, then make your request known unto God. Tell God that it is time for you to go on a journey that only He can take you on and then after that conversation, *rest* in Him. Allow Him to do what He does best (save, rescue, renew, restore, prosper). You are not so far gone or so deep in your stuff. God can handle it, if you let Him. Now be clear, it will require your participation.

DISCLAIMER:

DON'T ALLOW YOUR MIND to mess with you. If you are anything like me, you will begin to try to figure out how to fix all the mess you are in. Stop and rest, Jeremiah 29:11 NKJV says it like this, "For I know the thoughts that I think toward you, says the LORD, thoughts of peace and not of evil, to give you a future and a hope." Ladies, He knows how to fix, change and adjust everything in your life so that it lines up with His plan. Your only focus should be spending time with Him and in His Word (understand that the two are truly one). It's in Him that you find yourself! Love you ladies!

CHAPTER 3

No More Joy Riding

..

LET ME WRITE ON the canvas of your imagination for a minute. Imagine a Saturday in spring, the temperature is about 70 degrees and your day is completely clear and free. You decide to just go for a ride with the windows down, sunroof back, shades on and music playing. Sounds good doesn't it?

Lets' do one more. Imagine your 17 year old daughter comes to you and says that her male friend asked her to hangout on Saturday and would that be ok with you? You ask her, "Where are you all going?" She responds, "I don't know, he just said, "hang with me." Does that scenario sound as appealing to you as the first one? Probably not.

Well, don't be fooled, the scenarios are packaged differently but have a very real similarity. They have no destination. You must be very careful when it comes to presentation because the enemy will use his same old trick. He simply packages something in a way that appears to be more appealing but the destination is the same: steal, kill and destroy boulevard! Neither example has an identified destination. That's exactly what joy riding is. It is getting in a car with the understanding that we are just going to enjoy the ride regardless of where we end up. Where is the true joy in that, would you tell me? As believers, we must use the wisdom and knowledge that God has so freely given to us. Ladies, the days of joy riding must end. Okay, let me dig a little deeper. You met a man six months ago, what is the identified intent for the relationship? What do you want to give and get from it? Is the man in agreement with the objectives? Has the purpose or intent even been discussed or are you just going for the ride with the hopes that you will end up where you want? So often, women struggle with the feeling that speaks and says, "I don't want him to think that I'm pushing him or pressed to be in a relationship because I'm not, so I didn't say anything." Well, lets' go a little further. You and this same man have now been joy riding for a year and now your feelings are involved. You decide to ask him, "What are we doing?" and he responds, "we're friends, we're chillin, having a good time." Now you are ticked off! Not his fault ladies, sorry! You jumped on that ride without valuable information. You gave the impression that you too were just "joy riding." Oh and this is the one I have grown to hate with a passion. "I'm just going with the flow." What in the world? Let me meet the person who created that cliché. The only flow I'm going with is the one led by Holy Spirit. If the leader of the flow has a name like Kevin, Mike or James, I apologize, I'm not going! Why? The Word instructs me to be led by the Spirit of God and not by my flesh. See, that flow is a set up for heartache and heartbreak because women want to be loved, honored, protected and provided for. We were not created to just randomly "flow." Because of this, the real you will eventually kick in and switch gears on that man. The time will come when you are ready for the flow to cease. Now, I understand that there are seasons in a woman's life when she may not be ready for an exclusive courting relationship with a man and that's fine. However, that does not negate the fact that when she is in her season of being ready to receive her gift from God, trust me, you want a man that is destination driven, not joy riding! Ladies, we must have those conversations and sooner than later. I have never gone on a job interview and been told "we just want someone to come on board and go with the flow." What? No, the purpose of the interview is to identify if you are a good fit based on the objective the company has for that position. They have already identified what they need to be successful and what qualifications they believe are required from the person holding that title. Following that, they begin the process of screening potential candidates. I think it is a phenomenal system. So ladies, why have we encountered men, agreed to go out with them and yet avoid the important questions that serve as key determining factors? Enough is enough with these bootleg screeners. Just because he is fine, well groomed, has a nice smile, gainfully employed and arrived to the meeting place in a very nice luxury car does not mean he is exempt from the screening process. Even friends must be screened whether you are in your season of waiting to be found or just simply establishing healthy friendships.

Let me further engage your imagination for a moment. Ladies, every public transportation system has an identifying routing number, letter, name or color (C22, Green Line, etc.). These identifiers help the traveler connect the mode of transportation with the destination. Let's take a bus for example. The bus number may be C22 and it may have 14 stops on its route. It has a starting place and a final destination. How many times have you just randomly boarded a bus not knowing where it was going? Probably never. Why? If it wasn't headed where you were going, then it would simply be an inconvenience and waste of your time. Well ladies, we must look at our social lives like that. We must be purpose driven women, strategic in our dealings and careful concerning those people that we choose to entertain on any level. This means that we cannot be overly concerned with what others will think as a result of our inquiry. If a man cannot handle the questions then there is a clue right there. Now ladies, I'm not saying to introduce yourself and then ask, "Do you love Jesus? Do you want to be married? What is your purpose? What is your relationship like with your Mama?" What I am saying is that your screening conversation must happen quickly. This will determine if the person meets the criteria for establishing a potential friendship.

Ladies, I am not sharing something that I read about. I am sharing what I lived for a significant period of my life. I am grateful to God for the blueprint to being a successful single woman. I cannot keep this information to myself, you are my sister girls! I am bothered when I see beautiful, intelligent women in these relationships that are going nowhere. These relationships that are a clear indication of them settling for less. I watch and listen to stories of women who have been with men for a number of years, had babies, lived together and yet they aren't married. The part that bothers me most is when I know that the women want marriage but settle for being the live in girlfriend. They settle for doing life as the girlfriend but serving as a wife. Basically, being pimped instead of honored. However, this only happens, if it is allowed to happen. Women, we have to maintain a posture that causes us to always submit to Holy Spirit because He will lead, teach and correct. Therefore, if you stayed in that relationship for nine years and he didn't marry you, it isn't because God didn't speak, you just didn't listen and obey. We serve a loving God, who always has our best interest at heart. He will make it crystal clear when we need to flee a situation, or better yet, embrace one. He loves His daughters. My issue used to be hearing but not obeying and wow, there are consequences for that! Ladies, no more of that life! We are daughters of Christ, submitted to His Word and the promises and principles in it. We are precious in His sight and deserving of the honor suited for queens. That is our inheritance, so we can no longer accept or live common lives. So, return your "joyriding license" and allow God to chauffeur you around this thing called life. Sing with me, "Aint no God like the one we got, no one can do it better!"

You deserve purpose filled friendships and relationships with individuals who compliment and support who you are in Christ. You are not just another chick. In Biblical times and even now, people of royalty live by different standards than those considered to be common folk. Establish your lineage in Christ, if you are a believer then you are an heir of Christ Jesus and if you aren't, then daughter it is time to make that decision.

Okay, now you're probably thinking, "That sounds good and I understand, but I have been with him for three years now or we already live together," or "I already love him and it's going to hurt too bad to walk away," "We have talked about marriage," "We have kids," "He just wants to get his finances together," "He's just going through a lot right now," "He just needs me to be there for him" – are you seeing a pattern here? There are always going to be reasons or better yet "excuses" behind why you won't do it God's way. I purposely did not say can't because you can. The power of choice allows us that. The real question is, does settling hurt more that the pain of walking away? Does accepting the situation "as is" hurt more than making a decision that you deserve God's best? Yes, the chances are that hurt will be present, but I can guarantee you that not living God's best hurts way more. These are our lives ladies and we don't get a "do over." We are living out our days with every breath and what we do today is setting up our tomorrow. It's time to put the big girl panties on and make some big girl decisions. I can remember a minister saying years ago that sometimes you must press into the pinch because if you pull away from a pinch it hurts more. That's so true. You may have to make some drastic changes that cause you to feel hurt, confused, lonely and upset. However, always remember that feelings are like light switches, they turn off and on. They aren't permanent and that's why we shouldn't rely on them or be dictated by them. The Bible says, " I say then: Walk in the Spirit, and you shall not fulfill the lust of the flesh" (Galatians 5:16 NKJV). The flesh will set you up every time. The flesh is deceiving to say the least, but God will not let you down. This journey will cause you to trust Him at another level. Things won't always make sense, feel good or be as planned as you would like, but "He knows, what He is doing." Ladies, these lives we live are not about us. We are here for a purpose. My existence is about ministry. It is about honoring God through my lifestyle and Him being able to use me to win others to Christ. As a result, I can't just think about myself when I make choices because my choices don't affect just me. Everything I do or don't do affects someone else. Why? Because there are people assigned to me. People that I am called to educate, empower and serve. Living holy prior to marriage isn't just about me, it's about my children, your children, you and all those assigned to reap from my decision. My decision will serve as an example to someone else that it is possible. It will be a voice spoken in a world that isn't speaking, teaching or living this principle. If I would have given up and decided that I couldn't weather the storm, then there would be no book, workshop or conference. Likewise, with my marriage. Marriage for me isn't solely about companionship or even good sex (you caught that, "good sex", confession is powerful). Marriage for me is about ministry. I want God to use me as an example of what a godly wife looks like. Ladies, this life is not about us going to work, stopping at the store, dropping the kids off, taking a summer vacation and eventually getting a retirement check. There is purpose residing on the inside of us. We are here to make a deposit in this earth. Therefore, the choices we make either compliment the purpose of God or work against it. How you walk out your life is being watched by someone else. Your children, family members, friends, coworkers, etc. are watching you. Is your life serving them any good? Can the demonstration of how you're living help them draw closer to God or will it push them deeper into their present level of below-average living? Making a decision to have purposeful and God designed relationships is bigger than you. Embrace that concept today. God has something awesome waiting for you. He's not working on it, doing it or trying to figure out what to do concerning your life. It is already done! His work is finished. He is simply waiting for you to trust Him enough to walk with Him.

ASSIGNMENT:

TAKE A QUIET MOMENT to think about your current situation, whatever that might be. Have you just been going with the flow? Does your social life lack God-given direction? If your answer is yes to either of these questions, then it is decision making time again. Life is full of decisions. Begin to search the Word of God for God's criteria concerning being in a friendship or courtship. Write this information down. This will help you in determining who qualifies to be in your circle.

DISCLAIMER:

DON'T GET WEARY. As you begin to learn of God's criteria, you will begin to see that very few might qualify. No worries. This is God's way of protecting His precious daughters. Not everyone qualifies to be your friend or husband and as you grow in Him, you will appreciate this more and more. You don't want company. You want God-approved friendships and companionship. You can find company anywhere!

CHAPTER 4

Where Do You Bank?

••

I AM A VALUED member with a few banking institutions. Prior to becoming a member, I performed adequate research on each to help in making a well informed decision. I looked at interest rates, monthly maintenance fees, reputation and history. After doing such, I completed the application process and was welcomed into the banking family. There is however one thing that would keep me from banking with an institution. That one thing is: unequal transactions. Let me explain. If I make a deposit and return at a later date to make a withdrawal and the exchange made is not equivalent to the deposit, then I'm done. Follow me to the bank for a moment: Good Morning, I would like to make a withdrawal. I fill out the withdrawal slip with all required information and provide the teller my driver's license and bankcard. I am requesting $10,000 dollars. The teller begins logging the information in the computer, goes to the back and returns with 10,000 coupons. What in the world just happened? Unacceptable! I made a deposit that exceeded $10,000 dollars prior to that day. I attempted to get $10,000 dollars out and did not receive anything close to what I put in or am due. Don't leave me ladies, I'm going somewhere and I need you to go with me. That would be a major problem for me. I don't know about you, but I'm feeling a scene from "Set It Off." Under a scenario as such, I could no longer bank with that institution. There would be no second chances, no justifying their behavior, and no statements easily taken similar to, "Well, the bank got cheated before and so sometimes they just do things like this." Sound familiar? Come on ladies, we have been there before. My membership would immediately end and my lawsuit would begin simultaneously. Why? I made a deposit and expect to receive what I gave. See the Bible says it like this, "Do not be deceived, God is not mocked; for whatever a man sows, that he will also reap (Galatians 6:7 NKJV) It's a law and if there is a breach in the law then there is a real problem! Listen to this statement, ladies, and let it settle in your spirit: "No more Emotional Investments and Painful Withdrawals!" The Bible instructs us to guard our hearts. If I could tell you how long I socially banked with that institution, it would blow your mind! How many times was I going to emotionally invest and get the same painful outcomes without examining the root of the matter? Now, the physical descriptions changed on the people, but the spirit remained the same. The name might be different, complexion a little lighter or darker, height changed and personality differed, but contained the exact same spirit every time. Yet, I continued making the emotional investment. We are emotional creatures by nature. That's how God created us and we need not apologize for that. The Word of God declares, "I will praise You, for I am fearfully and wonderfully made; Marvelous are Your works, And that my soul knows very well." (Psalms 139:14 NKJV). There is purpose in us being emotional creatures. How do I know? Because we serve a purposeful God. He did not make a mistake. The caveat to this is that we must learn to manage our emotions. Unfortunately, a lot of us are not taught how to manage our emotions and so we do as we "feel." The enemy is also aware of this information and he attempts to play on us in this very area. No worries because, "You are of God, little children, and have overcome them, because He who is in you is greater than he who is in the world."(1 John 4:4 NKJV)

We must make a deliberate decision to learn how to manage our emotions. This includes knowing how to guard them, knowing when you have the green light to release them and learning to own them, but not be led by them. Here are some examples: I'm ticked off but I choose to guard my response. I'm unclear but instead of assuming, I ask questions. Instead of nagging about something, I pray about it. I might be feeling you but I am not going to be calling you consistently because I have not heard from God concerning you. Now you're following me. When these steps are not followed, we find ourselves experiencing cycles of painful withdrawals in relationships. We wanted marriage; we wanted love; we wanted the long term and we got something completely different. We received infidelity, babies out of wedlock, drama, wasted time, heartache, heartbreak, debt, and stuff that we did not sign up for! It's time to end that cycle and begin living in that next dimension of social freedom in Christ. This requires emotional management and we are going to examine this closely in this chapter.

When God began revealing this to me, I started hearing and seeing things so differently. I remember having a conversation about this with my accountability partner and she shared something so profound and accurate that I must share. She said, "The first investments that men make into women are through their time and money, yet as a proceeding response to these efforts women invest their hearts and bodies." Not the same investment. After she said that I saw it like a movie, literally! I saw a man who recently met a woman and they started going out on dates that he paid for. They were together almost every moment. He was clearing his schedule and making TIME for her. He was bringing flowers, cards and cute tokens of interest. After a few weekends of this, the woman started feeling "some kind of way." Ladies, don't play me, y'all know what I'm talking about. The woman started feeling him emotionally. When her girlfriends asked about him, she blushed and had that silly little look on her face. All of what she was experiencing was in response to some time and money. The very same things he gives his male friends. Follow me to my second visual. It's Sunday night and the game is coming on. Mike calls Darryl and says, "Hey, we watching the game tonight at my house, come over, oh, and bring some wings and ice." Darryl is about to invest his time and money. Ladies, just because he is investing his time and money that does not mean he qualifies for your heart and body! Men operate differently than we do. Don't mistake their attempts to get to know you for you being the one! That same time and money he spent on you, he spent on Lisa and his boys last month. Women, our hearts are like our children, they deserve our protection. I'm a mother and am very protective of my children but for a period of time I released my heart to those who did not qualify. Just like I am protective of my children, God, Our Father is protective of us. Slow down ladies. What I just described to you is what I have termed Premature Emotions. Let's look at the concept of prematurity. It is the term normally used when a baby has not reached full maturation or refers to an act done before its proper time. On occasions when babies are born premature they are sometimes required to stay in the hospital in the Neonatal Intensive Care Unit (NICU). This is for the purpose of monitoring them. In a lot of cases, they may be underweight, have difficulty breathing and just experience some challenges due to not reaching full term development prior to entering into the world. As a result of these factors, they are closely monitored to assist with any existing complications or to prevent complications. Now, speaking as an educator, we have also been taught that premature babies are more likely to experience developmental delays. Now, as a believer, we don't operate based on facts, we operate based on the truth and truth is found in the Word of God. So any parents with 'premature babies' – don't panic. The Word of God calls them healed and I stand in agreement with that Biblical promise for your children. This information is merely being used because we are going somewhere with this. So, if we liken the factors that the medical and education field have identified with the emotional realm, then let's look at this from another lens. If as women we prematurely give our emotions to relationships that have not been screened, observed and approved by God, then it is almost a guarantee that there will be complications or delays. Why? because it wasn't time or it wasn't for you. The relationship had not come to full term where you were given the green light of approval from God, your Father. If without caution, you send emotions prematurely into a relationship, you will experience emotional sickness. But, we call it disappointment, heartbreak or settling. As mothers, or even those soon to be mothers, we desire healthy babies that go full term. We understand the benefits connected to maturation when in the womb. Likewise with us, before we enter into these relationships, God wants us to reach full term in our singleness. He wants us to experience that point of maturation that happens from being in the Secret Place of the Most High. He doesn't want us to go out before our time. He knows what the world will attempt to infect us with. He does not want us to experience any complications or delays. Oh, but once we know who we are in Him and understand how to manage our God-given emotions then we are something to be reckoned with! Y'all, I have a very vivid imagination and so I saw the acronym NICU (Neonatal Intensive Care Unit) while sharing that example and immediately after, God showed me SPU (Psalm 91:1) and explained that to be the Secret Place Unit!! Yes! That's the place where God your father, friend, doctor and everything else you need Him to be resides and monitors you. You have a place that you can go to learn how to experience success as a single. In the interim, I am going to share with you the keys that God revealed to me that contribute to premature emotional investments in the next chapter. God has given me a blueprint for how to live holy, experience peace and receive the promises that are due to me through Him. Just hang in there with me; I got you because He got me! As He gives to me, I am obligated by assignment to give it to you.

Emotion by definition is a natural instinctive state of mind deriving from one's circumstances, mood, or relationships with others. We also call emotions, "feelings." We as women were created with the gift of being able to feel. We cry when we see other people cry; we can watch a movie and literally "feel" what they are experiencing; we can see a "mess" and "feel" for the person in it. These feelings however can serve us or hinder us. God being our creator and father understood this about our gender and, because of this, He reminded us in His word, not to be led by our flesh or better yet our "feelings." Feelings can overshadow wisdom and understanding if we allow it. Lets look at it practically. When you met him, you knew that he had a lot of things he needed to work on in his life. You saw it from day one. However, as women, we have the ability to see that one good thing that is in operation in his life. Listen, we say things like this, "but he has a good heart, he's so considerate, he's so helpful, etc." and it is during those moments that emotions can lead or wisdom can lead. Wisdom might say, "This is not a friendship that you should actively pursue," but emotions might speak and say, "Oh, but he's a good guy and he just needs to be around some good people that can help him." Okay, now those things might be true, but you must be crystal clear that you are called to be one of those people. Every good idea is not a God idea. Know the difference. See, what starts off as you just being cool with the "guy," with all the issues, can quickly turn into a three-year relationship with someone who never qualified to be in a relationship with you. It is then that you are required to pick up the pieces and deal with the residue from that relationship. Wisdom could have prevented that. I am compassionate by nature. That is how God created me. I "feel" people, especially those in rough places in their lives. I have been like this since I was a child. I want to help everybody and a part of my call is to help those in rough places, but ministry and forming personal relationships are different. It took me a while to realize this. I have served in the field of special education for many years. I gravitate to students with major issues, especially behavioral. I was created for them. I am able to see beyond their behaviors. God allows me to see the root of the matter. Well, because of this I "feel" differently about them than others. Well, my mother who was a 30+ year special educator made a statement one day during my years of extreme chaos. She said, "Stop bringing work home." I was confused at first. She shared that the very area I served during the day was the same area I was gravitating to in my social life. I looked back and realized, oh no, 90% of the people I dated were emotionally disturbed. Seriously, ladies, every man I dated, needed my help. They needed my counsel, encouragement or assistance in some way. I was indeed the counselor girlfriend. That was not only the farthest thing from God's best for me but nobody was really able to pour into my life, give me counsel or wisdom. Everybody seemed to be two minutes from a crisis whether they realized it or not. I was emotionally giving myself to these people and looking back at it now, what could I get in return but a painful withdrawal? That is all they had to give at the time. Ladies, as we grow in Christ, we become more equipped with determining who can stay and who must go. Guess what? Some good people with good hearts will have to go, because if where they are in their lives can pose a hindrance to us, then they don't qualify at that time. God is a loving and protective father. Everybody doesn't qualify in His eyes and as a result, they can't in ours!

ASSIGNMENT:

ASK YOURSELF THE FOLLOWING questions: Am I emotionally investing in people that I shouldn't? Do I invest without God's approval? Am I quick to "feel" and find myself resisting wisdom? If your answer is yes to any of the questions then do a few things: Ask God to terminate any soul ties and eliminate any unhealthy connections that you have to anybody. Then, ask God to begin to show you the things that cause your emotions to be prematurely invested. Last, if you are in a current situation where your heart is involved and you know that God is not, then ask God to show you the way to exit. Get out of it ASAP! I Corinthians 10:13 NKJV says, "No temptation has overtaken you except such as is common to man; but God *is* faithful, He will not allow you to be tempted beyond what you are able, but with the temptation will also make the way of escape, that you may be able to bear *it*. There is an available EXIT!

DISCLAIMER:

EMOTIONS ARE LIKE ROLLER coasters – they take lots of turns, loops and drops. During this time, your emotions might be heightened. You may become more sensitive than ever. Whatever you do, don't turn back. Just like they come, they go. You keep your eyes on God's Word and confess that you are led by the Spirit and not the flesh. This too shall pass!

CHAPTER 5

The Dating Game

··

LET'S PLAY A GAME. My mind would be a terrible thing to waste because as you can tell I see in color and am not afraid to color outside the lines. Open your mind and imagine being in these three scenarios.

I'm going to present three possible scenarios that you can pick from that exist behind door number one, two or three. Are you ready? Great!

Scenario 1: You meet a man named Tony and he says to you after introducing himself, "Hi, I'm Tony. I think you are absolutely gorgeous. Your body is sexy and you have a very pretty smile. When I saw you, I was immediately physically attracted to you, so I'm definitely going to be working on having sex with you. I just recently got out of a relationship and am not looking for anything serious right now but if it happens, it happens. I'm going to be very diligent in the beginning with calling you, texting and spending time with you. I am also certain that you will love the attention and will begin to have sex with me very early. I will want you to periodically cook, boost my ego, help with my kids and do considerate things that demonstrate that you are into me. I do want you to put me first but I don't want you to have that expectation of me because I'm still going to continue my life as usual. After that initial period of trying to get you, my efforts to maintain the friendship will dwindle because the hunt will be over and I will be bored. We will begin to argue, disagree and I will start being attracted to far more women than when I first met you. After a few vacations, spending a couple holidays together and wearing that bedroom action out, I will want out. I will share with you that I'm not really ready for a relationship. It seems like I can't give you what you want and I'm going to move on. After about a month, you will hear from a girlfriend that I'm back with my old girlfriend and we're getting married. It's not time to pick; we have two more scenarios to choose from.

Scenario Number 2: You meet Davion and he is okay. You aren't instantly attracted to him but he is funny. After listening to a series of jokes you decide to give him your number. Davion calls the next day and says: "Okay, this relationship is going to go real slow because I haven't been in a relationship in a long time. I was locked up for a while and so I'm trying to rebuild my life. What I really mean is, I'm trying to make up for the lost time. I hang out with the fellas a lot and I'm a serial dater. Being locked up ain't easy. I am going to try my best in the beginning. I will try to impress you because I feel like you're out of my league, but since you went for those tired jokes then I will try my hand. I will eventually introduce you to my family, make extra adjustments to spend time with you and I'm going to really take an interest in you after a while. I have a very catering mother so I am going to expect you to be the same. I normally eat out and I don't really manage my money well but I'm a good dude. I'm not really goal oriented and could see myself just living "as is" for a while. I'm that complacent man. I don't have any dreams or goals outside of my 9-5 and chilling on the weekends. We will do this relationship thing for about four years. After about nine months, I will stop using a condom because I'm going to tell you that you are my woman and I'm not seeing anyone else and I love you. You will be led by your emotions because you don't seem to be emotionally stable so it will work on you. In another four months you will get pregnant. I'm going to tell you that keeping the baby is your choice but I don't think I'm ready. I'm ready for the sex, your cooking, cleaning, support, encouragement and assistance, but not kids. About a year after our son is born you will get pregnant again and I will give you the exact same speech as before. After experiencing the demands of the kids, I'm going to realize that this is just too much for me. You are going to really be in love with me by now and I will love you, but not enough to marry you or even continue in the relationship. I will then tell you that we need to go our separate ways because I'm just not ready for moving in with you or marriage. I will then leave you to figure out what life looks like as a single parent. I will contribute both financially and my time, but other than that you need to figure out how to raise two kids without a family unit. I will thank you for the four years of life that I used, but that's how the relationship will end. So, which one sounds most appealing to you or do you want what's behind door number three?

Scenario number 3: "Hello Sweetie, My name is Kevin. I am the guy that you will end up falling for despite knowing that I really don't compliment you spiritually. I'm going to do the very basics, treat you decent and try to do this "God" thing with you because you say you are a Christian. I also know that you aren't going to let me go quickly because I am detecting a bit of a low self-esteem. You also seem real needy. You are going to be really impressed with me because I have a successful career, demonstrate maturity and independence as a man and I'm fine. I don't do the church thing but I will tell you that I am spiritual. You will eventually make excuses for us being unequally yoked. You will make it seem as if my relationship with God is something that it really isn't. The fact that I am willing to go to church with you and have conversations about God with you really pulls you in. Yes, you will tell me that you don't want to have sex and I will tell you, "no pressure." Little do you know, I am still going to try to have sex with you and I'm still going to live my life like I was before meeting you.

I will continue to see and have sex with other women. I'm going to do this as long as it works for me. You will eventually break down and have sex with me. This will begin to wear on you because you do have a relationship with God and want to live right, but your self-esteem is in such a place that you will accept me regardless. You will eventually get hurt because I'm going to get tired of the back and forth about what's right and wrong in the eyes of God. Some days you have sex with me and other days you are preaching to me about how you can't do it anymore. I really will get tired and will want you to pick a side and stop faking. I will start becoming really annoyed with your emotions. I told you we were just friends anyway. My calling, texting and seeing you will begin to fade to almost nothing. You will call me one day crying, telling me how you trusted me and thought I was different and how could I do this to you. I will be trying to figure out "do what to you?" I will remind you that you are grown and made this decision. I will tell you that I didn't force you to entertain me, like me or have sex with me. I will remind you again that we are only friends. After this conversation you will never hear from me again. I won't even answer your calls when you attempt to periodically check on me. For what? I will be done with you and I won't look back. It was nice while it lasted and I hope that church thing works out for you."

Ok ladies, which one sounds appealing to you? Scenario one, two or three?

Ladies, as much as these scenarios were placed in a game like format for the sake of making a point, these types of options are silently chosen every day. A woman is picking one of the listed doors every time a woman chooses to play wife with the title "girlfriend." Every time you choose to place your heart, body and soul on the line with no attached covenant you are choosing one of those doors. The only difference is that he isn't telling you from the introduction and I'm not blaming the man! That's right! We are responsible for our actions. If I went on an interview and the interviewer told me, "Look, we are interviewing for a teacher but we will only give you the salary and benefit package of an educational assistant," I would exit that interview immediately. Would you agree to that? I doubt it because I surely wouldn't do it. It's no different than women playing wife but being the girlfriend. This is not the plan of God. Once again ladies, I lived this and for too long! And some of you are still living it. This is what that dating game looks like.

What is dating? Dating is a free for all. I get to enjoy you with no real covenant. I tell women all the time, you are either SINGLE or MARRIED. You have never filled out paperwork that has "go together" by a box to check. Why? It's not real! Dating is a game. It falls under that umbrella of "joy riding." It's risky, it welcomes premature emotional investments and it creates an atmosphere for temptation and sexual immorality. There isn't normally any accountability or supervision with these encounters or relationships. Both parties are just going with the flow. These relationships normally have as their purpose, "to have fun, get to know you, etc." Very rarely is marriage discussed as the reason behind getting to know the other party. Dating is a destructive game and should be proceeded with caution if chosen to do so. I now subscribe to "friendships or courtship." There aren't even any biblical references of dating. That was not jumping off back in the day! If a woman was found to be randomly entertaining a man that was not her husband, she was considered a Ho! They didn't say Ho, I said "Ho" – they called her a whoremonger. Same thing; different day. Why? There was an order to having an interest in the opposite sex. You didn't just act on your interest. Families were involved among a host of other things. Nowadays, a man may not meet your family until after three to six months of you all being together. By then, you probably already gave him some and are emotionally invested. You didn't present him to anybody for their advice, counsel or wisdom. Dating is too independent and does not make room for submission to an outside covering. When I was dating, I can remember a girlfriend telling me that what I was doing wasn't safe or wise. She started to explain to me that I was meeting men, going out with them, getting to know them, spending time at their houses and them at mine. She said, "Nobody knows them." Nobody knows when you are out with them, where you are going or anything about them except you. She said, "Anything could happen and nobody would know where to start because you are just doing what most grown women do, just dating!" My ignorant response at that time was, "Girl, I'm good." It was nothing but the grace of God because looking back now, she was absolutely right. Day by day nobody knew who I was with or what I was doing and that was unacceptable living. Guess what I know? I'm not the only one who was living like that. Some of you still are. We are entitled to God's best and that isn't it. I'm a mother and under no circumstances would I give my daughter approval to live like that. No Ma'am. Ladies, we are so valuable to the Kingdom of God, our daughters, other women and to men, but we have to understand our worth. There must be standards and principles in operation in our lives. When did we decide to adopt this worldly idea of how women operate in relationships? Who convinced us that the "live together" or what I call "test drive" was an acceptable option? A man asking, "Can you all live together" is not an exciting offer, it is a demeaning one because what he is really saying is, "I think you're good enough to try out but not good enough to buy or invest in for the long term." You are allowing him the option of making or denying the purchase after he has used the merchandise over and over and over again. WHAT? No ma'am! This one is the absolute silliest statement I hear, "We're talking about getting married" Really? Seriously? Y'all live together, raising kids together, paying bills, you are having sex and spending your life in this relationship and you all are now talking about marriage? Silly talk! Imagine going to work on Monday and your supervisor said, "I know we hired you, but we want to see your work for about a year before we decide if we're going to pay you." You would be out the door! You would not allow them to use you and then decide if they are going to pay you. Likewise with a man. God showed me clearly that a man does not have permission to use his daughters in a wife-like capacity without a marital covenant. However, His daughters must be the ones to enforce and live by this standard. Enough is enough! We aren't common and cannot continue to live according to common standards. Okay, while I'm at it, let me destroy the thought process that says there is a certain time period that exists for being sexually intimate with a man. No Ma'am. Show me that in the Word of God! It does not exist. God does not say that after thirty days, six months or one year, that the criteria has been met for sex. You are out of the will of God if you sex him day one, day thirty or day one hundred eighty. God's word states that that we are not to participate in premarital sex! For clarity, premarital means anything prior to marriage. So let's abolish attempting to mix man made concepts with Biblical standards. It's like telling God, "I want the blessing but I also want to do it my way. "No servant can serve two masters; for either he will hate the one and love the other, or else he will be loyal to the one and despise the other" (Luke 16:1 NKJV). If you have decided to follow Jesus, then let's live according to His manual, the Word of God. When we truly allow God to show us who we are, then it almost becomes insulting when someone expects "common" from us. I take pride in my abstinence now. I'm grateful that I can stand before my own teenagers, both young and older women and men and say, "I made a decision to live according to the Word of God and because of this I will remain abstinent until my wedding day." I'm not like everybody else and so I cannot operate like everybody else. There was an article online recently about a basketball player taking a picture with a royal family and in the picture he put his arm around the woman. The royal community was in an uproar. Well, I didn't think about the scenario in reference to them, but I did think on it in reference to women of God. See, the community was in an uproar because they hold the royal family to another standard and because of that there are things that cannot be said or done in their presence and touching was one of them. Call me Queen KeeBe because I can surely relate. That's how our Father, God looks at us. The spirit realm gets in an uproar when we are not being dealt with properly. Why? I am a part of the royal family. The Bible says, "But you *are* a chosen generation, a royal priesthood, a holy nation, His own special people, that you may proclaim the praises of Him who called you out of darkness into His marvelous light;" (1 Peter 2:9 NKJV). We are responsible for teaching people how to treat us. We must show them what works and what doesn't work; who can stay and who must go. Ladies, it's time to take our rightful positions and stop playing. Keep yourselves (mind, body and spirit), wait on God and you will be found.

Now, I'm sure you are wondering, 'If I'm not supposed to date, then what can I do concerning the opposite sex?' I'm so glad you asked. Here are two categories and they are: friendship and courtship. Let's examine friendship and we can look at courtship in the next chapter.

By definition a friend is a person whom one knows and with whom one has a bond of mutual affection *absent* of a sexual relationship. On the other hand, affection is a gentle feeling of fondness or liking. So, being a friend is really having a reciprocal relationship where two people are fond of each other and that fondness is not clouded, distorted or manipulated by any sexual interaction. It's when two people take the time to get to know each other and then they identify a value for each other based on what they learn and experience with one another. The Bible instructs us as believers to interact with each other as brothers and sisters outside of marriage. Therefore some of the stuff that happens during most dating relationships is definitely off limits because that would not go on with a brother or sister. If so, we have another issue on the table!

The friendship "relationship" is often skipped over and never really established because so often people go right into dating. So, what is needed to establish and maintain a healthy friendship with someone of the opposite sex? Glad you asked. Knowledge of who you are in Christ, boundaries, standards and agreement. These things must be in place to establish healthy friendships with men. First, you must identify if the man wants a friendship and what friendship looks like to him. Unfortunately, we live in this era where society talks this "common" foolish language that says that there are things called "friends with benefits." No Ma'am! That's dating and he is just really emphasizing to you that he doesn't even want to pretend like you all are in a relationship! A friendship doesn't have sexual benefits because sex is not in the equation so NEXT! Once you identify his idea of friendship, you can then determine if his standard meets the criteria for developing a friendship with the awesome woman of God that you are. You may have to decide that he doesn't qualify. Most importantly, you must determine what the blueprint looks like for being in a friendship with you. This relationship resembles that of a brother and sister. It is limited in its' interaction. You all don't "pretend" like you are a couple. I was famous for that one. I required men to act like they were with me whether we were dating or not. Y'all know I had issues, stop playing. You respect each other's lives and space. You don't communicate with a mandated consistency. Meaning, if he doesn't call you for a couple of days your face isn't in a knot. You aren't questioning what's going on or even upset. You maintain an amount of space that is conducive for a friendship so that you don't send mix signals or set the stage for a shift in intent. You limit private socializing. You socialize in public and in groups. This eliminates the appearance of wrong doing and eliminates unnecessary temptation. Remember ladies, we are more vulnerable and comfortable with our friends and, therefore, having a friendship with someone of the opposite sex can be tricky and a set up for disaster if not managed properly. As women, we are emotional. We value people who are genuinely interested in us, pure in their intent and who appear to have no strings attached. This makes it very easy for our feelings to change towards the men we initially intended on just being friends with. So be very mindful and careful. This is why time, space and settings must be monitored. A friendship with a man can be a great thing, but ladies use wisdom so that you are really building a friendship and not dating under the title of a friendship. This too can be a formula for disappointment if you don't manage your emotions and you make a shift in your desires for the relationship and he doesn't. So, proceed with caution and in all you do, honor God!

Once I surrendered to a journey of locating myself, I also looked around. I realized that the majority of the women I knew or were in my circle at that time had unhealthy and dysfunctional relationships. I did not see one relationship initially that I would have wanted to mirror or follow as an example. I saw baby daddy drama, live together chaos, single women sexing like 40 going north, the "I will take him because he works, has a house and a car"– all types of scenarios that caused me to say, "Oh no." I knew that I was on the wrong road and needed to take the closest exit. I had to separate myself from all examples of foolishness. The Bible says," Do not be deceived: "Evil company corrupts good habits." (I Corinthians 15:33 NKJV) I don't even watch television shows that model chaos, trashy living or could contaminate my spirit. I no longer want to be entertained by the very stuff that God hates! That stuff is contagious and I want no part of it. I was already a mess and I had to detox from it all. That was another reason I started connecting more with my parents. I wanted to surround myself with those that were living holy, not compromising and demonstrating something worth imitating. I am destined to have a friendship, courtship and marriage worth imitating! Well, guess what? I have some really great news for you – the same applies to you but only if you make the decisions necessary to experience those things.

ASSIGNMENT:

IF YOU HAVE EXPERIENCED some God-given revelation after reading this chapter and believe that you too will eliminate the category of dating, then congratulations. I welcome you to this great place. I would now encourage you to continue searching the Word of God so that you are clear about what to give and expect in friendships and courtships. If you are currently in a dating relationship that has no identified destination, then jump ship! You are better than that and deserve better. Love you ladies!

DISCLAIMER:

YOU MAY FIND YOURSELF spending a lot of time alone. It is okay and purposeful. God does not waste moments. Embrace the time. It is during those moments that you will begin to learn and enjoy your own company more. I will be good company to my husband because I have learned to be good company to myself!

CHAPTER 6

All Rise, Court is in Session

..

YES MA'AM, YOU GOT it correct, it's time to discuss courting! This is the portion of the relationship that can follow the development of a healthy friendship. Once those two people have established a healthy friendship, either party or both may initiate the conversation about the potential for courting if their thoughts about the person or relationship have changed. Disclaimer: all friendships don't turn into potential courtships. Some friendships will start and stop at just that, friends! And it's okay! It is possible for the people in the friendship to begin to desire a long-term relationship with one another and, if so, a courtship is explored.

Courtship has been defined as a relationship between a man and woman in which they seek to determine if it is God's will for them to marry each other. This relationship excludes romance and sexual activity. Once again, no sex! – you're getting closer though.

Let's really look at some practical pieces included in the courtship process: the man and woman are both believers of Jesus Christ and they are willing to submit to a "covering couple." A covering couple will provide accountability, supervision, guidance and wisdom during the courtship process. The man and woman will diligently seek God concerning His will for them concerning marriage. They will monitor and limit their interactions to avoid premature emotional investments and clouded judgment. They will continue to interact in public and in groups. They will monitor and limit private interactions. They will keep the relationship neutral enough that if either party decides to go their separate way, it is easy and with little to no effect. They will proceed with establishing a true friendship.

Okay, now since we have covered some very practical pieces, let's put this into real scenarios.

When a couple meets and decides that they are interested in courting this does not include "boo loving." My young people taught me that. I love young people; they assist in keeping me young. This means, you all aren't communicating all day and night, spending every moment together, holding hands, kissing and caressing. You do, however, spend time participating in settings and activities that support your interest and provides opportunities to get to know each other better. This does not mean sitting all cuddled up on a Friday night watching a movie in an empty house. NO! Run for sexual purity sake – seriously. Ladies, as you embrace your journey, God will teach you triggers and things to personally avoid. I tell women all the time, God helped me to identify the fact that I am not a nighttime chick. I don't do dark unless supervised. Once the sun begins to go down, it's not a good look for me. I am atmospheric. I enjoy tranquil atmospheres, dim lighting, candles and soft music. Well, understanding this about myself allows me to set a standard that says, "I will not entertain under those conditions so that my sexual integrity is protected." This lifestyle changes how we are accustomed to doing things. Yes, we are adults, but adults submitted to the Word of God. This means that how we socialize and get to know people differs from that of the world. No worries, you will still have fun, get to know each other and honor God all at the same time. It's also very important to remember that while getting to know each other, you are also laying a foundation for your potential relationship. As women, we have been created to help, support and bring honor to our potential husbands. Our existence in their lives should assist them in becoming closer to Christ and not pull them away. Therefore, if we are doing anything that assists in persuading them to compromise in their relationship with God, then what kind of foundation is really being laid? And are you really wife material yet? Marriage is a covenant relationship and we are in a covenant relationship with God. If God requires us to live according to particular principles and we agree and then don't keep them, what is to say that we will keep them in marriage?

I have a concept that I truly believe now. If a man or woman chooses not to crucify their flesh and remain abstinent until marriage to honor the covenant with God; then once married and tempted by another man or woman, what will make them honor the covenant with the spouse if under pressure? I'm not convinced they will. The ability to crucify your flesh must be developed just like other areas and remaining abstinent is a true developer (trust me). The way a courtship is carried out is a true testament to the foundation that is being laid for that potential marriage. What better way is there to bring glory to God and demonstrate to your potential spouse what you have to offer as a godly wife –a.k.a.- virtuous woman?

I personally selected my parents as my covering couple. They have been married for 20+ years, love Jesus and have a very blessed marriage. Therefore, when I do enter into a courtship, I am prepared to have them oversee it during the process. Ladies, having a covering couple is so important for the sake of submission training as well. I had lived a single, independent life for so long that I had to freshen up on submission all over again. As a single woman, I did what I wanted, when I wanted and did not run my decisions past anyone.

Therefore, when God started to really work in me at another level, I purposely decided to set myself under my father as my covering. This means if I would find an interest in someone, I don't just act. I sit down and discuss this with my parents and get their feedback. We pray about it and then my father shares whether he gives the green light or not. This was new for me because I had never lived like this. I am also being trained in submission so that when "Mr. Right" identifies me as his "Good thing," I will cause him to obtain favor with the Lord. The Bible clearly states, *"He who* finds a wife finds a good *thing,* And obtains favor from the LORD." (Proverbs 18:22 NKJV) YES! I am very prepared for that process to be highly supervised and strategic. This is truly a blessing to me because I am not doing it alone. I have parents that are seeking God on my behalf, willing to supervise my courtship process and provide counsel along the way. Now, I must admit that I have fun parents so them going along will never be a problem for me. I told y'all, they are already in my social circle so they never cramp my style. I am also clear that because I honor the covering relationship, if they were to tell me that they are not in agreement with a potential relationship, I am prepared to submit to that as well. Submission doesn't just apply when we hear what we want. If you place yourself under the care of a chosen couple that you believe is living holy, submitted to the Word of God, hears from God and has a marriage that honors God, then you must be prepared to submit regardless of what you feel. God is faithful and when your heart is purposed toward Him, He will not allow you to be deceived by the enemy.

Remember, it's he who finds a wife, not a boo thang, girlfriend, friend with benefits or the like. If you believe you are in a season of being found, then don't focus on being found! Confusing? Focus on allowing God to prepare you as a wife. When your husband finds you, you should already be wife material. I now know that I am truly being developed as wife material. My parents and pastors have trained me well and my husband to be will have a confidence and clarity in Christ Jesus that I am his wife! There will be no doubt residing in him as to who I am!

ASSIGNMENT:

FOCUS ON GOD – NOT BEING FOUND! God knows where you live and He will make sure that your husband finds you when the time is right! If you are already in a courtship process, I would encourage you to practice some of the steps listed above if you are not already doing so. Love you ladies!

DISCLAIMER:

THE UNCOMMON MAY APPEAR frustrating, over the top and too unfamiliar to you. Well, remember that you are expecting an uncommon, over the top blessing from God. We reap what we sow. Therefore, if I sow the uncommon, I will reap the uncommon. I don't want what I see from the majority of relationships or marriages in this world. I want that God thing that surpasses what the finite mind can conceive.

CHAPTER 7
Retired TDC

••

I'M NOT REALLY INTO cars. I like what I like and that's it for me. If I have determined that it's something I would look good in when driving then the car has passed the initial test. Well, I have come to learn a little bit about the sell of cars that intrigued me. For a very long time, I assumed, which is never good, that the showroom cars were off limits for driving. I thought they were model cars – just there for viewing purposes only. Well, after research, I was taught that any car on the lot or in the showroom can be driven by an interested customer. I was floored. After that information was shared, I had a lot of questions like: how do you protect the mileage since they lose value the more miles they have? What qualifies a car as new/used if they can all be driven? What is the purpose of a demo car if the rules for used cars apply to them as well? Questions, Questions, Questions! Well, the very patient dealers answered all of my questions. I was informed that as cars are transferred from the headquarters they are driven to the ports that ship them. Therefore no car will arrive at a dealership with zero miles. Then they shared another nugget that got my attention even more. I was told that there is one condition that is an exception to the rule. You can order the car through the dealership but want it straight from the factory. Once it arrives nobody is allowed to test drive it because it belongs to you.

Now, for every reader, sister girl or friend that was wondering what Retired TDC stands for, it means **Retired Test Drive Chick**!

Praise Break: Hallelujah! That's right. There was a time in my life and maybe yours where you allowed yourself to be test driven. See, the concept behind a test drive is: the driver gets to test out the vehicle however many times he or she wants prior to making a decision whether or not he or she wants to buy. He or she can add extra miles and wear and tear and then decide if he or she wants it or not. Well, that concept works at dealerships and unfortunately has been working in the lives of so many beautiful single women for far too long. Okay, what is a Test Drive Chick? It's when a woman decides that she will award a man the "wife benefit package" while allowing him time to decide if he wants her as a wife. It's when he gets that unlimited sex card. It's when women decide to play house with a man that isn't her husband. It's when a woman allows a man to call her girlfriend or even friend and yet she performs almost all the wifely duties. TEST DRIVE CHICK! Basically, woman are silently saying, "You can put as many miles on me as you want and as much wear and tear as you like and when you are ready, let me know if I have been approved for your wife." Oh, you don't like to hear it like that but that's what is being said through consensual actions. It also says that he deserves more and you deserve less. No Ma'am! Every day, women are allowing the world to tell them that men deserve to try out your sex, live with you to see if you all are a good fit, establish bills and even have a few children in the interim and it's okay to give him time to decide if that is what he wants. Unacceptable! We are God's daughters, not TEST DRIVE CHICKS! Everything on a car lot can be test driven from the newest car to the oldest. The only car that cannot be driven is the one preordered from the factory and that's because it is just for the customer that purchased it. Well, well, that's the order of God. God is clear that when His daughters are found, it is likened unto them being pre-ordered from the factory. If a man is not willing to enter into a covenant with you based on hearing from God and desiring to spend his life with you, then let him go! Give him wings. Once that man has gone before God and made a request for you and followed the proper steps to receiving you as his bride, then you can do all the riding and driving that you like – but not a minute before. You're a factory chick, straight from God's factory and because of that, men *Can Look But Don't Touch!* You are a perfect fit for that special man and when he finds you, he will find you living holy. He will also meet you down the aisle the same way he found you, untouched!

Let's cancel out the mindset that states "he can get it." I hate that term. He doesn't qualify to get it! How about that? Just because he's nice and spent $4.00 on a sandwich does not mean that he deserves to lay down with you. So what he makes you happy? If you made yourself happy prior to him, then him making you happy wouldn't hold as much weight in your life! Women have allowed these worldly standards to penetrate their minds. A man does not deserve to be intimate with you just because he is fine or because you never met anybody like him before. He definitely doesn't deserve to "get it" because he has a few dollars. His house, cars or lavish gifts don't mean anything when it comes to your value. You are priceless! A man doesn't deserve to get it because he is nothing like the last man, talks about God and goes to church. So What and Good for Him! He needs to go! We ALL need to go. He doesn't get any points for going to church. If the mindset has shifted to thinking that what a person gives qualifies them to have you, then that is very similar to prostitution. For those ladies, money is what they must get to give it up. For others it may be attention, a few dinners, some loaded compliments and a few gifts. Ladies, attend to yourselves and what he brings to the table will simply be an extra and not a necessity! You won't feed on that attention like some starving wildlife animal. Jesus paid it all, so don't put yourself on sale. You are not a discount chick. "You were bought at a price;" (I Corinthians 7:23 NKJV). Don't reduce your value because of an urge you feel in the midnight hour or the fact that he really seems to be a great guy. Great guys want sex too and will take it if you're giving it! You are worth more than that, but until women begin to realize that, the liquidation sale that is happening in the world will continue.

Okay, now you're thinking, 'I understand what you're saying but I'm no virgin, so how does this work for me at this point?' The Bible says, "Therefore, if anyone *is* in Christ, *he is* a new creation; old things have passed away; behold, all things have become new." (II Corinthians 5:17 NKJV) Just as the odometer on a car can be turned back, God is in the renewal business. Ladies, all you have to do is repent and turn from your wicked ways. Key: repent and turn! If you have been compromising yourself sexually, then turn, which means stop. If you are playing wife, in an unhealthy relationship, settling and waiting on a man that has been giving you the run around, turn and walk away. Your Father God is waiting to receive you, clean you up and get you back on the right path.

Sex is meant to be beautiful, holy, enjoyable, fun and a pure demonstration of love within a marital covenant. Don't believe or buy into the lie anymore. Sex is more than just two physically attracted people, sweating and demonstrating their creativity in bed. It's not something that can be done without any repercussions. For every cause there is an effect and for every decision we make or seed we sow there is a harvest. Don't be fooled into thinking that it's over just because you didn't get pregnant or an STD. The Bible says, "Flee sexual immorality. Every sin that a man does is outside the body, but he who commits sexual immorality sins against his own body" (I Corinthians 6:18 NKJV). There is more going on during sex then you realize. God wants it done in His will so that you and I are under His divine protection. Ladies, we will no longer open the door for the enemy in our lives. We don't want that spirit to operate in our bloodline anymore. We will live as women of God and raise up generations to come that will also live under that same standard. Unfortunately, sexual activity is happening at an alarmingly young age now. It is common to find elementary aged students experimenting with some level of sexual activity. That is unacceptable. However, if that is the standard and spirit in operation in front of them, then what should we expect? Children deserve better examples and to see that there is another way to do this. The Bible says, "There is a way *that seems* right to a man, But its end *is* the way of death" (Proverbs 14:12 NKJV). Generations to come need us to rise up and live according to principles worth imitating. God's command to us as singles to refrain from premarital sex is not designed to punish us, but to protect, prepare and position us. God our father is a protecting God and because He knows the end from the beginning, He knows what's waiting for us when we operate outside of His will. The enemy's objective has not changed. It is to steal, kill and destroy. However, we must not give the enemy any room to work with in our lives by blatantly disobeying God's order and will. There is a blessing in obedience and God desires to prepare us. This preparation is not just for us, but those connected to us. We are called to be witnesses of Jesus Christ, His representatives on the earth. If we are His disciples but don't live according to His will, then what are we good for? Time out for claiming Him, but then living just like the world. When people look at your life do they see anything different from those who don't claim Jesus? And I mean beyond church attendance and you saying spiritual clichés like, "God is good, all the time," "I'm blessed and highly favored," or, better yet, "I'm blessed by the best." Come on ladies, people should look at our lives and see Christ because of how we live. Your potential spouse should be able to say that he has never met a woman like you because of how you live for Christ. Trust me ladies, your life can change at this very moment if that's what you desire. My pastor always teaches us that "we live and die by the choices we make" and that's true. Make a choice to live holy; make a choice to be different; make a choice to trust God and resist the way the world does life. God will never let you down. He can take you from Ho-iness to Holiness! However, God is a gentleman. He will not force change on you. Ladies, trust God with your social lives. Trust God with the selection and timing of being found by your husband. Trust God that He can keep you from sexual immorality and present you to your husband brand new.

Oh, and let's not forget positioning. In our single years, God has commanded us to live holy because He is also positioning us. When the Bible talks about a man finding a wife, it is because she is already wife material. She lives and operates like that Proverbs 31 woman. She crucifies her flesh, she has purposed in her heart to be faithful over the covenant that she has established with God, she honors her word, she submits to God and accountability, she is diligent with meditating on the Word and she is clear that she was chosen by God. These things develop and mature us as women of God. There is a big difference in a girlfriend and a wife. God never called us to be girlfriends, but there is a maturation process that happens with being prepared and positioned to take on the role of a wife. Becoming a wife is bigger than getting a ring and changing your last name. Women are having that experience daily, but not all of them are living as wives. God has called us to be wives according to His standards. We have been called to set an example for the world as to how the marital union should be. However, this doesn't just happen. It happens on purpose because we decided to be deliberate and intentional in being developed, trained and matured for taking on that role. So, stop looking at rings for a moment and spend some time in the secret place. Put your bridal book to the side and pick up the Word of God. Stop daydreaming about the wedding and start meditating on how you are going to operate as that Proverbs 31 wife every day of your marriage. I'm not saying there is anything wrong with those things, but our focus should be on allowing God to work on us while we are single so that when our day comes we are indeed protected, prepared and positioned for our new role in the earth. Let's meditate on stuff like how patient we will be with our husband, how our words will always be used to build him up, how we will always be faithful and submit to him. Come on now – let's meditate on things like that. I always tell my girlfriends that my wedding can be however my husband wants it to be because that is really not my focus or interest. Weddings last for a day, but I am investing in having a fruitful marriage that pleases God and is enjoyable to my spouse. I don't spend my time looking at rings or dresses. Once again, there is nothing wrong with that, but just not my focus at this time. Forget how pretty I'm going to be on that day; I'm going to be "two dollar" cute regardless. My desire is to be that uncommon wife that creates a life and atmosphere for my husband that causes him to want to run home every day of his life. So, ladies once he gets me and you see him smiling, you will know why. He will be able to confess that I was indeed worth the wait!

ASSIGNMENT:

Make a decision right now that you will stop sexing, fornicating, ho-ing, rolling, tricking, "THOT-ing," whatever you call it and you will turn to God. Make that declaration to God, find someone that will hold you accountable and stay in the Word of God. You can't go wrong with the Word. Love you ladies!

DISCLAIMER:

Just because you have made this commitment, that does not mean you will not be tested or tempted. You might have days where you wished that these were not principles found in the Word of God. Rely on the Word of God, stay away from environments that create temptation. Guard your senses. It ain't nothing like a man that smells good, looks good and sounds good, but there is truly nothing like the favour and blessing of God on your life and that's what we are entitled to! So get yours!

CHAPTER 8

Single University

••

How much more could we emphasize the importance of education? We live in a world that is constantly sending the message that education is key. Those of us who are parents "drill" this very same message into the heads of our children. Why? We understand that knowledge is critical in preparing us for successful living.

I have been in the field of education for more than 15 years and the most common question I hear people ask children is, "What do you want to be when you grow up?" Now, this answer varies from child to child. I have heard everything from "a princess to an archaeologist." I must be honest, I personally like that princess thing because if she truly gets the revelation, then her life will differ from that of common women. However, with the many answers I have heard, I notice that most educators have a common response to those answers when talking with teens. The follow up response is, "Do you know what is required to be that?" Let me tell you how I can remember asking my daughter when she was in middle school if she had an idea as to what she wanted to do when she got older. Her response was, "I want to be a judge." Okay, you already know my follow up response, "do you know what is required?" This chick answered, "I don't know, I mean I know you have to go to college." So, me being me, I asked, "When do you think you want to start finding that out?" This chick didn't have a clue. I started sharing what was required and she was amazed. Well, that is not just common for teens. How often do we as people decide we want to be something or have a certain position or status in life but don't have a clue as to what is required of us? The Bible says, "For my people are destroyed from lack of knowledge." (Hebrews 4:6 NIV) In high school, counselors typically begin to diligently work with students to help them identify what they are interested in and they support them in placing them on the track for whatever the choice is.

I don't know what happened in my case. As a child, I decided that I wanted three things when I grew up. Don't laugh; I'm sensitive. I wanted to be a hairstylist, psychologist and own a McDonald's. I made that decision at age seven. Well, in high school I came up with the bright idea that I wanted to be a marine biologist so I could swim with the dolphins. I enjoyed being in water and I think dolphins are just so cute. I mean, that is how you pick a career right? I started college, declared my major and began taking classes. I looked at my schedule and I was taking all of these science-based classes. Wait a minute – I was confused. When do we get to learning about the habits and behaviors of sea life? When do we intern at Sea World? I took those classes for my first semester and realized that I didn't want this as a career. I just wanted to swim and play with some dolphins. Well, bless God, a few years ago I swam with some dolphins in Jamaica and loved it. I'm satisfied! That first semester could have been used differently if I would have taken the time to identify ahead of time what was really required to be a marine biologist. The process should go as follows. Identify what you want, research it to identify what is required and then study to become it. Once you have your eye on the target you must consistently and constantly make deliberate and intentional efforts to access information to be what you set out to be. This isn't a one-stop shop. This becomes a lifestyle of "being." This is the rationale behind professional development. It allows opportunities for those currently in their careers the ability to access more information. My pastor has always taught, "if you

can't define a thing, you can't be it." Follow me; once again, I'm
going somewhere.

There are various stages in life and in those stages there are
different responsibilities, requirements, patterns of thinking and
behavior that can cause that stage to be successful or unsuccess-
ful. Let me make it practical. The law states that at 16 years old it
is permissible to hold a driver's license and drive an automobile.
Well, it is also required that a driving class is taken so that future
drivers will not only have the physical skill of driving, but the
information needed to carry out that function in a way that is
safe and beneficial for themselves and others. Their thinking must
line up with their new position called "driver." The law doesn't
say, "oh you are sixteen, here are the keys." Training and teaching
must happen. Let's switch lanes. When children attempt to do
or request things that are outside of their stage in life, adults will
sometimes say, "No, you are not grown." This statement is made
because whatever they are requesting is outside of their scope of
thinking, behaving and stage in life. Therefore, as parents it is our
responsibility to teach them how to be successful in their current
stage. We train their thinking with the intent that their actions
will line up with the train of thought. The Bible says, "train up a
child in the way they should go and when they are old they won't
depart from it." (Proverbs 22:6 NKJV). This process and way of
life should be applied to every stage. Watch me now. We are single
women, but are we freestyling our way through? Whether you
chose this position or just ended up in it again, you are here so
enjoy it and embrace it according to the Word of God. There is
a way of thinking, behaving and overall living that has already
been outlined for us in the Word of God. This way will allow us
to live abundant lives as single women. However, if we are not
constantly learning and meditating on what God has spoken concerning this position in life, we will not prosper in it. The Bible
clearly speaks on matters like what the condition of our hearts

should be, what we should be confessing, how we are required to conduct ourselves with the opposite sex, our finances and the list goes on. The Bible does not leave one stone unturned, but if we aren't in the Word, then, yes there is room for discouragement, fear, insecurity, worry, lack, sexual immorality and the like. God has called us to live abundantly and if we are in agreement with that then we must do the work to acquire that life. He has already done everything that He is going to do. He sent His son, we have the Holy Manual of Instructions (Word of God) and Holy Spirit. Now it is up to us whether or not we will utilize what we have been given to be successful singles. You study to become! There is a confidence that follows being educated concerning a topic. This happens because we feel a sense of certainty in relationship to the information we have acquired. This information in any area equips us in the natural. Now if we mix these same natural steps with spiritual principles for prosperity as singles, we cannot fail. Success is guaranteed. We will no longer be hearers of the Word but truly doers! You can always gauge an area of deficit based on what you're saying. The Bible says, "Out of the abundance of the heart the mouth speaks." Begin to listen to what you are saying. When you hear yourself making statements like, "Ugh, am I ever going to get married? Are there any good men out here? Maybe, I do need to lower my standards, are there any men out here that will honor the principle of abstinence or better yet living it them-selves?" Those statements represent your spiritual diet. You are simply regurgitating what you are feeding on. Where do those thoughts come from? Could it be the shows you watch, the mes-sage in the music you listen to or the company you keep both male and female? A thought worth exploring. Now are those thoughts possibilities for some? Absolutely, but not for us as believers or at least it should not be! That's the problem. Believers are settling for the outcomes designed for unbelievers. However, if you begin to feed on the Word of God concerning the area of "singleness," those previously mentioned statements turn into statements that resemble this: "No good thing will He withhold from me as I walk upright before Him," "I know that I will be married and have a fruitful marriage because the Word says that if I delight myself in Him, He will give me the desires of my heart," " He knows the plans that He has for me and they are to prosper me and not harm me, to give me a future and hope." You get my drift. Feeding our spirits with the right diet is easily identified in our language and our actions! The Bible says, "Man cannot live by bread alone but by every word that proceeds from the mouth of God." We must know what God says about our lives in these areas. This applies to every area, however, we are discussing our singleness so that's the focus at the moment. This same principle will apply when you transition into the position "wife." If you are not learning from the Word of God how He called you to think, speak and behave, then you will not have a prosperous marriage. This is a lifestyle, not steps we simply take to get something! We are cultivating our relationship with God. In this, He teaches us how to conduct ourselves in our current position to reap the very best. How does one graduate without learning the mandatory principles and then demonstrate the application of them? It is then that graduation is attained. As an educator, if students cannot demonstrate that they have both acquired the knowledge and can apply the information, then retention is inevitable. We will not be retained, settle for less, live average or mundane lives. We can do this ladies and in a way that pleases God, blesses us and is a blessing to others.

Well, I'm not satisfied with just being single because I am entitled to more according to the Word. I want successful singleness and not based on the standards of this world. The world will tell you that if you are attractive, educated, have an excelling career and a host of material things then you are a successful single. Well, I know otherwise. I know that those things don't give you peace or joy. Those things can't save you, rebuke you, heal you, give you grace or forgive you. Now, don't misunderstand me, those things are great to have but they don't lay the foundation for successful living. Our relationship with God lays the foundation for us to be able to handle and enjoy those things that are considered additional blessings. Therefore, that relationship requires investment just like any other relationship! It requires quality time, learning Him and honoring the principles identified in the Word. Whether you like it or not, there are things that can be done by some and not others. There are things that kids can do that teens can't, adults can do that seniors can't, singles can do that married people can't and here is the BEST one – there are things unbelievers do and say that believers cannot! This is not a bad thing ladies! These are the principles that, if acquired and applied, set us up for graduation to the GREAT life! Those things are the "added onto" that is mentioned in the scripture. The Bible says, "Seek ye first the kingdom of God (God's way of doing things) and His righteousness and all other things will be added unto you." As we make our relationship with God the priority, we will indeed get the desires of our hearts. So, I ask you the very thing I had to ask myself: Are you educating yourself in your relationship with God on how to be a successful single or are you freestyling? The Bible is clear when it says that we reap what we sow. If I don't sow into being a successful single woman, then I sure better not be looking for the harvest of one! So ladies, if you have not already been doing so, it's time to enroll. It's enrollment season! The only requirements are your book (The Word of God), your time and the application of what is downloaded in your spirit. Successful Singles University is accepting applications and you have already been accepted! Just start your full time journey! Side note: I do believe that learning to successfully live as a single will also assist in preparing you as a bride. Do life God's way!

Let's do a quick recap of what is being recommended: Take an inventory of your successfulness as a single, begin to study the

Word of God concerning the various areas involved, spend quality time communing with God and meditate on that which you have studied. Now for clarity, the entire Bible is a holy manual given to us and is beneficial in its entirety. However, I suggest that you study the Bible based on what your needs are at the time. Prime example: if you are struggling with fornication then don't study tithing, study and meditate on scriptures that pertain to living holy in your flesh. P.S. Don't read the Bible, study it! Don't treat it as something on a "to do list" that you can check off of your "I'm a good Christian list." Eliminate the mentality that says, "I read my Psalm and my Proverbs and I'm done." That is not to say that God will not speak through those scriptures, but there are even more nuggets that He will give you concerning where you are at this very moment if you avail yourself to those moments through His Word. Make sense? Perfect. Lastly, I did not mention this, but this is key. It matters what church you attend. Make sure that you are in a Bible believing and Bible teaching church. Church partnership should not be based on where you grew up, who attends or what's closest to the house. You must be in a church that can meet your needs according to what God has for you. It is not surprising that God led me to be a partner of Spirit of Faith Christian Center with Drs. Mike and Dee Dee Freeman. I am in the right place and at the right time. I am submitted to leadership that can train, develop and impart into me what is needed for me to fulfill the plan of God on my life. We all require that, so make sure you are in the right church, for the right reason and at the right time.

ASSIGNMENT:

STUDY THE WORD OF God in the areas related to single living!

DISCLAIMER:

DON'T GET DISCOURAGED IF you sit down to study and it appears difficult, you lack focus or you all of a sudden get sleepy. Those are the typical and predictable attempts of the enemy. Just don't stop. Start studying and meditating on the Word of God. If you study that same scripture all week or month, fine! As you apply the time and consistency, God will definitely speak to you and those previous distractions that were mentioned will fade. Remember, the enemy stays on his job, so he has to apply pressure to attempt to keep you from the Word. Even he is aware of the power of the Word in a believer's life. So, press forward and get yours! We win in every area of our lives.

CHAPTER 9

Matchmaker

..

LADIES, ALLOW ME TO *assist with introducing you to yourself according to the Word of God. It's time you met your perfect match and she resides inside of YOU! You must meet her before you meet him (the husband)!*

Hello, My name is_____ (fill in your name) and I am fearfully and wonderfully made and marvelous are His works. I am beautiful, intelligent, gifted and here on purpose.

I am created in God's image, I am His clone, His earthly employee and representative. I have dominion over this earth and authority resides on the inside of me. I am unstoppable because if God is for me, then who can be against me? I am the righteousness of God. I was bought with a price and I honor God with my body. I don't allow, entertain or embrace people or situations that would tempt me into a place of compromise. I meditate on the Word day and night and am careful to do what is written in it. I am holy because He is holy. I am a chosen people, a royal priesthood and a holy nation. As a result, I don't live by the common standards of this world. I have rejected their formula and submit to the principles in the Word of God. Greater is He that is me than he that is in the world. I am powerful, capable and here on assignment. I can do all things through Christ who strengthens me. I am the salt and light of the earth. So, when you see me, you are seeing in 3-D. You are experiencing the Father, the Son and the Holy Spirit in me! Proceed with caution because an encounter with me can be life changing in your favour! God is at work in and through me.

PRAYER OF SALVATION

Dear God in heaven, I come to you in the name of Jesus.
I acknowledge to You that I was born a sinner and I
repent of my sins. I acknowledge that I need you.

I believe that your only begotten Son Jesus Christ shed His
precious blood on the cross at Calvary and died for my sins.
I also believe in my heart that he rose from the dead.

You said in Your Holy Word, Romans 10:9 that if we
confess the Lord our God and believe in our hearts that
God raised Jesus from the dead, we shall be saved.

Right now I confess Jesus as the Lord of my life. This very
moment, I accept Jesus Christ as my own personal Savior
and according to His Word, right now I am saved.

Thank you Jesus for your sufficient grace. Transform my
life so that I may bring glory and honor to you alone.

Thank you Jesus for dying for me and giving me eternal life.

Amen.

Congratulations sister, you just made the best decision of your life!

NOTES

Thank you ladies for allowing me to share my journey with you. It is my prayer that you will live in a manner that pleases God all the days of your life. We have a great work to do on this earth.

XOXOXOXO

WWW.KEEBESMITH.COM
P.O. BOX 711
UPPER MARLBORO, MD 20773-0711
240-326-3770